Full Court
Control Basketball:
A Flexible Offense to
Exploit Opponents' Weaknesses

DICK GEYER

PARKER PUBLISHING COMPANY, INC.
West Nyack, N.Y.

Dedication

To my parents, Dr. and Mrs. H. G. Geyer
To my wife, Mary Ellen
To my children, Tom and Betsy
To the late Msgr. Paul J. O'Dea
To Coach Jack Ryan
To Coach Jim Devine
To Coach Bob Telerski
To Coach Mike Irwin
To the fine young men I have had the privilege to coach

Library of Congress Cataloging in Publication Data

Geyer, Dick,
   Full court control basketball.

   Includes index.
   1. Basketball—Offense. 2. Basketball coaching.
I. Title.
GV889.G49   796.32'32   77-2964
ISBN 0-13-331736-6

HOW THIS BOOK CAN HELP YOU

The biggest change in basketball since the jump shot has been the improvement and sophistication of today's individual and team defenses. This defensive revolution has been so far reaching that many coaches now claim that they spend 60% to 70% of their practice time on the defensive phase of the game of basketball.

I, too, believe that defense is important in basketball, but still it is only one phase of a great game, and I want my basketball players to enjoy the entire game, and so we believe in spending 50% of our practice time on each phase of the game. Our coaching staff puts a great deal of thinking into both offense and defense, because our goal is to establish a balanced system of play.

The purpose of this book is to present the concept of full court control basketball, a flexible offensive system designed to exploit any defensive strategy. The label, *Full Court Control Basketball* is not meant to imply a slow down, control type of attack, but, rather, it refers to a total offensive system that can attack the entire court and take advantage of whatever the defense might be trying to do.

Full court control basketball has been successful because it is based on sound offensive principles. Each of the offensive series, whether it is a fast break situation, an attack against full court pressure, or a particular series against a front court defense, revolves around the following principles, which no defense can consistently deny.

1. *Purposeful Movement*—this refers to movement of both players and basketball to create problems for the defense, and, which, if not defended properly will enable the offense to penetrate the defense, or will produce the uncontested shot. Any defense will look good against a stand around offense, but as soon as movement is added the defense will find its job a little more difficult.

2. *Lay Up Potential*—all of our offenses involve some type of penetrating movement with or without screens, which if not properly defended will result in the high percentage lay up shot.

3. *Jump Shot Potential*—I am a great believer in the effectiveness of the 15-18 foot uncontested jump shot as a most devastating offensive weapon. All of our patterns have this potential available. It is most effective when it occurs as an option following the attempted penetration of the defense, which usually produces a defensive sag. This defensive tactic now makes it possible to maneuver players, with or without screens, into the 15-18 foot areas for the uncontested jump shot.

4. *Low Post Potential*—in each of our offenses there is the opportunity to post the ball at various stages of the pattern, if the defense permits it. The low post area is a most difficult spot to defend, so by creating low post potential the offense is again pressuring the defense in a high percentage scoring area.

5. *Offensive Rebound Coverage*—no matter which option of the offense produces a shot, players are located in floor positions which will enable them to move into the three offensive rebounding areas which are located in the two low post spots and the middle of the foul lane.

6. *Floor Balance*—every pattern is designed so that one player is responsible for moving into the area between the top of the key and the center circle when a shot is taken. His responsibility is to prevent a quick break by the opposition.

These six offensive principles form the solid foundation for *Full Court Control Basketball*. On paper they sound impressive, but they must be put into practice on the playing floor by a group of basically average basketball players. Therefore, *Full Court Control Basketball* is not only a system of play, it is also an educational experience for these players, an experience that is aimed at teaching the proper reaction within the system, so that not only within the system of play, but within the players, themselves, there is an element of court control. The variety and flexibility of Full Court Basketball has made the coaching of this system a most enjoyable event year after year, and it is to be further noted that this same variety and flexibility has made basketball an enjoyable learning experience for the participants as well.

Here, then, is *Full Court Control Basketball*. I am sure that each reader can find something here to add to his own game style. However major or minor that addition may be, the result will be an increase in offensive flexibility as well as an increase in the enjoyment of the players. To defeat today's improved defenses, offense flexibility is needed, and as offenses become more flexible, the game of basketball will continue on to greater heights of enjoyment for coaches, players and fans. *Full Court Control Basketball* will give you something extra to add to your offensive arsenal.

Dick Geyer

CONTENTS

3. Attacking the Front Court Zone with the Regular Zone Offense *(cont.)*

Drills to Develop the Regular Zone Offense

Drill #1 guard exchange drill ● Drill #2 penetration drill ● Drill #3 reverse phase drill ● Drill #4 complete offensive pattern drill

4. Dominating the Front Court Zone with the Overload Offense ● 77

The Overload Offense ● Methods of Achieving the Overload ● Overload Phase of the Offense ● Reverse Phase of the Overload Offense ● Variations for the Overload

Fake overload ● Low post adjustment ● 1-2-2 offensive set

Drills to Develop the Overload Offense

Drill #1 basic overload drill ● Drill #2 foul circle drill ● Drill #3 overload reverse drill ● Drill #4 complete offensive pattern drill

5. Producing Decisive Results with the Sideline Fast Break ● 97

Theory of the Sideline Fast Break

Fastbreak principles

Shooting Drills for Building the Break

Drill #1 lay ups ● Drill #2 loose ball lay ups ● Drill #3 three lane jump shots ● Drill #4 three on none fast break drill

Ball Handling Drills for Building the Break

Drill #1 two lane passing ● Drill #2 three lane passing ● Drill #3 three man weave ● Drill #4 five man weave

Half Court Drills for Building the Break

Drill #1 rebound and outlet drill ● Drill #2 two on one half court fast break ● Drill #3 three on one half court fast break ● Drill #4 three on two half court fast break ● Drill #5 four on three half court fast break

Full Court Drills for Building the Break

Drill #1 three on two, two on one continuous fast break ● Drill #2 the fast break drill

Team Fast Break

Drill #1 five on five ● Drill #2 group fast break

1

CONTROLLING THE FRONT COURT MAN TO MAN WITH THE MIRROR OFFENSE

THE MIRROR OFFENSE STRATEGY

Our basketball teams see the man to man defense in about 70% of our games. Because of this fact, our man to man offense has somewhat more variety than our zone attack. The primary attack used against the man to man is called the Mirror Offense. It is made up of three offensive series which originate from the same basic set as well as from the same basic entry movement. By observing how the defense reacts to one of the patterns determines whether the same pattern will continue to be used, or whether the defense has left itself vulnerable to exploitation by another of the Mirror Offensive series.

Since the Mirror Offense is made up of three different series, each must be simple to teach, as well as simple to learn, so that they can be run at maximum efficiency. Therefore, each series is made up of three or four quickly run options, one of which almost always produces the good percentage shot. The Mirror Offense is thus based on flexibility rather than on a continuity style of attack, and so if the good percentage shot is not produced by any of the options, the offense is reset and the same series is run again. As you will see, the entire offensive series is easy to teach because only minor changes occur from one series to the other, but these minor offensive changes can pose major problems for the defense.

The three series of the Mirror Offense are called the Regular, the Reverse, and the Invert and each series starts from a 2-1-2 alignment (Diagram 1–1). The offensive guards maneuver to about six to eight feet off the top of the key, with the weakside guard (i.e., the guard without the ball) a step behind the line of the ball so that he is in position to receive a pass from the strongside if that player cannot get the offense started. Rather than trying to force the ball into an offensive forward who is being strongly overplayed, it is much easier to reverse the ball and start the offense on the other side of the floor. This is usually very effective because of the sag of the weakside defenders (Diagram 1–2). The high post sets up in the foul circle, just above the foul line, in line with the basket. Each forward lines up on the buffer zone on either side of the foul lane. We refer to the painted blocks which separate the first lane areas on the foul lane as the buffer zone (Diagram 1–3). The forward on the ball side of the floor is the strongside forward. The strongside forward's move to get open for a pass from the guard is a move along the foul lane for one or two steps and then a push off the inside foot to the wing area, which is the area in the vicinity of the foul line extended. This move of the forward is referred to as a 90 degree cut to get open. When the forward receives the pass he immediately pivots toward the basket (this is called squaring to the basket) and begins to read the defense. This sequence of the 90 degree cut to get open and the squaring to the basket is basic to the starting of all our man to man offenses. Now that the entry into the offense has been achieved we can now look at each series in detail.

The regular offense

The Regular Offense is considered our basic man to man offensive pattern. Our Freshman and Reserve basketball teams learn it almost exclusively. Complete familiarity and understanding of the Regular Offense is mandatory if the other series of the Mirror Offense are to become effective, because it is the defensive reaction to the Regular Offense which determines our offensive strategy. The Regular Offense has four options.

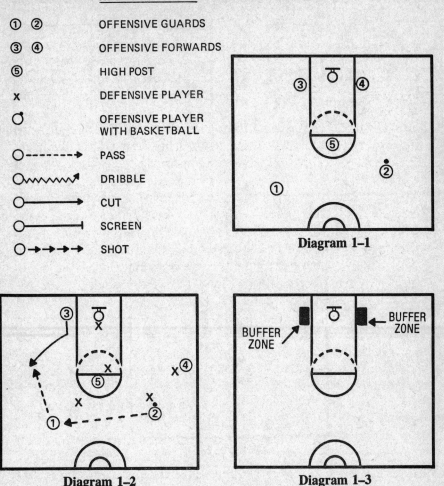

KEY TO DIAGRAMS

① ②	OFFENSIVE GUARDS
③ ④	OFFENSIVE FORWARDS
⑤	HIGH POST
x	DEFENSIVE PLAYER
♂	OFFENSIVE PLAYER WITH BASKETBALL
○------►	PASS
○wwwww►	DRIBBLE
○——►	CUT
○——┤	SCREEN
○→→→→	SHOT

Diagram 1–1

Diagram 1–2

Diagram 1–3

Option #1—*Give and Go*. O4 makes his move to get open. O2 hits him with a pass and makes a quick cut to the basket. This threatens the defense with immediate penetration and must be defended to prevent the lay up. If the cutter does not get the pass he continues through the lane, moves about halfway to the corner, and then returns to the top of the key for floor balance (Diagram 1–4). There are two important coaching points in regard to this initial offensive cut. The first coaching point is that the cutter must be aware of his defender and not commit an offensive charging foul which would stop the offense before it gets started. The second coaching point is that the cutter must always make a quick move to the basket, even if he gets a return pass only

15

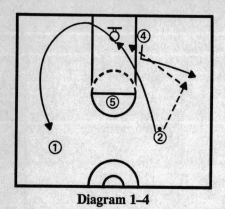

Diagram 1–4

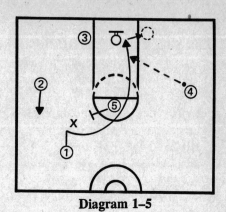

Diagram 1–5

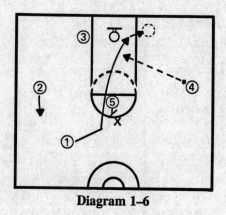

Diagram 1–6

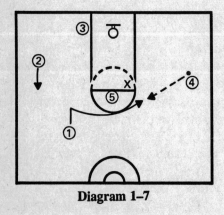

Diagram 1–7

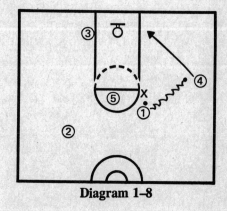

Diagram 1–8

once in a great while. The cutter must not get into the bad habit of cutting at only half speed. His offensive responsibility is to force the defense to work hard to defend his move or give up the easy basket.

On this entry into the offense we also expect the strongside forward to use a back door cut to the basket when he is overplayed, and to take advantage of a one on one situation if it is available to him when he receives the ball. Both of these situations must be recognized and exploited when possible.

Option #2—*Weakside Guard's Option Cut*. The second option of the Regular Offense is really three options in one, with the weakside guard reacting to the positioning of his defender. When the entry pass is made, the high post and the weakside guard begin maneuvering for the second option. The weakside guard starts to walk his defender toward the top of the key for the purpose of picking him off on the high post, who moves toward the weakside guard's defender to set a screen. The weakside guard will then make one of the three cuts, depending on the floor position of his defender.

Diagram 1–5. If the defender stays nose up on O1, he will cut over the top of O5's screen to the basketball looking for a pass. If the weakside guard does not get the ball he will set up in the strongside low post.

Diagram 1–6. If the defender moves ball side, O1 will fake ball side and cut behind O5's screen to the basket looking for the pass. If he does not receive a pass he again sets up in the strongside low post.

Diagram 1–7. If the defender sags into the foul circle area to deny the penetration, O1 moves over the top of O5's screen to the edge of the foul circle for the jump shot. If the defender recovers and the pass cannot be made, O1 will clear to the strongside low post. If O1 receives the pass but is unable to get the shot off, he will dribble to the strongside wing area, where he now in effect becomes the strongside forward, with O4 clearing to the strongside low post (Diagram 1–8). This maneuver enables the remainder of the offense to continue with no breakdown in the pattern.

Option #3—*Weakside Vertical Screen*. If no shot has developed from the cuts of the two guards, the Regular Offense quickly moves into its third option. As soon as O1 has made one of his three cuts, O5 releases from his screening position and moves down the weakside lane line to set a vertical screen for the weakside forward, O3. This is referred to as a "head hunting" screen, meaning that O5 is to search out O3's defender and impede his progress. Usually this defender will be somewhere in the lane area, so this screen must be set quickly to avoid a three second violation. O5 then sets up in the weakside low post where he becomes the weakside rebounder. O3 is coached to stay on the buffer zone and wait for O5's screen, then he breaks up the lane to the foul line to receive the pass. After receiving the pass he turns toward the basket (i.e., squares to the basket) and will take the 15 foot jump shot if it is open (Diagram 1–9). When O4 makes the pass to the foul line, he will wait to see if the jump shot will be taken. If it is, he will move to the middle rebound position. If no shot occurs, the passer holds his spot in the wing area.

Option #4—*Post the Ball*. When O3 gets the ball at the foul line, but cannot shoot, O1 in the strongside low post will move out to the corner. O5, who has set up in the weakside low post after setting the vertical screen, will now roll across the lane looking for a pass from the foul line (Diagram 1–10).

This option is also run if the ball cannot be passed to the foul line. In this case, O1 in the low post again moves to the corner, takes a pass from O4, and will attempt to post the ball to O5 rolling across the lane (Diagram 1–11).

If no shot has developed through these four options, the ball is brought out to the floor balance guard and the offense is reset. In resetting the offense we have used two methods, depending on our personnel. The simplest way is to have the players return to their original positions (Diagram 1–12), with the only change being that the two guards will have changed sides of the floor (Diagram 1–13). The other method is a type of rotation in which the original strongside forward moves out to a guard position; the original high post slides back across the lane and becomes a forward; the original weakside forward who moved to the foul line remains there as the high post; and the original weakside guard who moved to the corner slides into the buffer zone area and becomes the other forward (Diagram 1–14). The obvious advantage of the second method is that the defense is now forced into defending different floor positions than when the offense was first run (Diagram 1–15). Now with the offensive formation reset, the Regular Offense series is started again.

The reverse offense

The second series of the Mirror Offense is called the Reverse Offense. It is designed to exploit either of two maneuvers which the de-

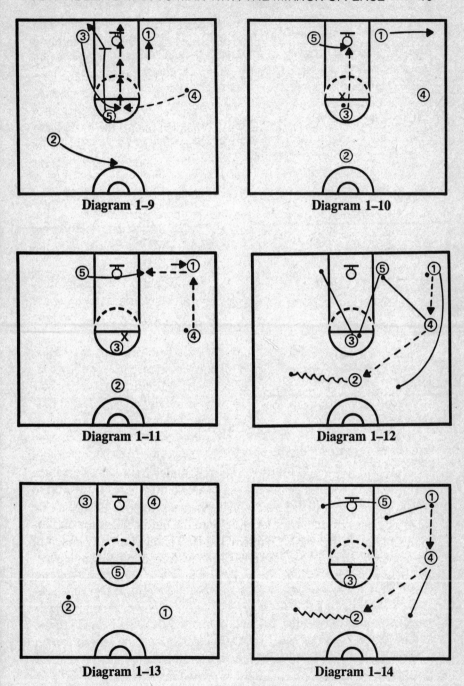

Diagram 1–9

Diagram 1–10

Diagram 1–11

Diagram 1–12

Diagram 1–13

Diagram 1–14

fense may employ against the Regular Offense. The first defensive maneuver that the Reverse Offense will defeat is the weakside forward's defender trying to anticipate the cut to the foul line for the jump shot. The second defensive maneuver that the Reverse Offense will exploit is the strongside guard's defender stopping in the lane to help out on the expected penetrating cut of the weakside guard. When it is recognized that either or both of these defensive maneuvers are being used, our team is instructed from the bench to change to the Reverse Offense. The Reverse Offense has three basic options.

Option #1—*Head Hunt for the Weakside Forward*. The offensive set and the entry movement into the Reverse Offensive is exactly like

Diagram 1–15

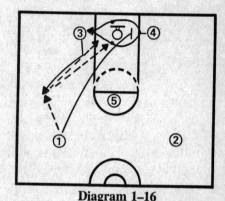

Diagram 1–16

the entry into the Regular Offense. The difference is that in the Reverse Offense O1 after making the pass to O3, cuts through the lane without looking for the quick return pass. Instead he looks for O4's defender, and he is responsible for setting a head hunting screen on this defensive player. O4 must wait for the screen and then break across the lane either over or under the screen depending on his defender's position. Ideally, the pass should be made to the forward as he moves through the lane. If he does not receive the pass he will continue across the lane and set up in the strongside low post and look for a pass (Diagram 1–16). This is a most effective option when the weakside forward's defender is anticipating the move to the foul line and will produce an extraordinary number of high percentage shots. If no pass is made to the cutting forward, he remains in the strongside low post. The screening guard will set up in the weakside low post.

Option #2—*Weakside Vertical Screen*. As in the Regular Offense, when the entry pass is made, O5 and O2 begin to maneuver into the screener and cutter relationship. However, in the Reverse Offense, O2 will always cut across the top of the key to the jump shot area. O5 after setting the screen, will roll down the lane as in the Regular Offense, and set his vertical, head hunting screen, but in this Offense it is for the original strongside guard, O1, who waits on the buffer zone, and then makes a cut to the foul line, exactly as the weakside forward did in the Regular Offense. If there is no pressure on O2 who cut to the jump shot area, the ball will be reversed to him, and he will then pass to O1 who has broken to the foul line for the jump shot (Diagram 1–17). If O2 is being pressured, he will move toward the sideline and O3 will make the pass to the foul line (Diagram 1–18). If a shot is taken O3 goes to the middle rebound spot. O2 is responsible for floor balance. This option is effective against O1's defender who has stopped in the lane to help out his teammates on the other cuts into the middle. Since he is concerned with helping out he is usually very easy to pin in the lane with O5's screen, and this will produce the uncontested jump shot at the foul line.

Option #3—*Post the Ball*. If nothing develops from the first two options, the offense now looks for the opportunity to post the ball. This phase is basically the same as the Regular Offense. If no shot is available from the foul line, O5 rolls across the lane looking for the pass. If the pass cannot be made to the foul line, then O4, who set up in the strongside low post, breaks to the corner, takes a pass from O3, and will try to post the ball to O5 rolling across the lane (Diagram 1–19). If

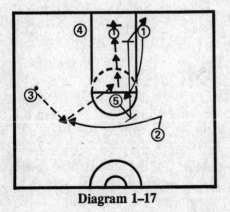

Diagram 1–17

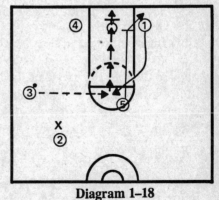

Diagram 1–18

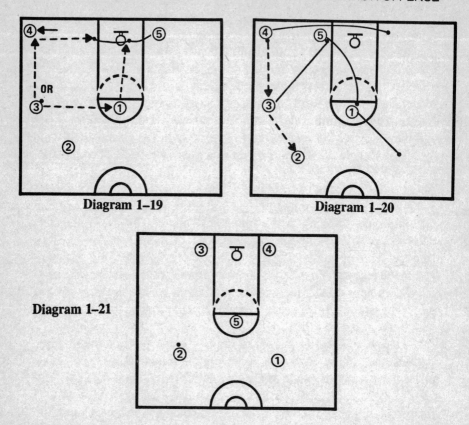

Diagram 1–19   Diagram 1–20

Diagram 1–21

the ball cannot be posted, the offense is reset. The Reverse Offense is reset by having the players return to their starting positions (Diagram 1–20), with the exception of the guards who once again, as in the Regular Offense, have changed sides of the floor (Diagram 1–21). Once the offense is reset the Reverse series is started again.

As you can see, the Reverse Offense is very simple, but the effectiveness lies in the fact that it exploits the defensive reaction to the Regular Offense. The offense knows that they are not running the Regular Offense, but the defense cannot be sure until the pattern is underway and they have been victimized with an uncontested shot, because they have reacted to what they expected the offense to do, when in fact the offense has done something different. Uncertainty has now been created in the defense by two simple changes in the offense. The defense will now begin to sense its vulnerability because it is unable to differentiate between the two offensive series, and whichever series they react to stop, their reaction can be exploited by the other series. The defense will now lose its ability to anticipate and that means that the offense is on its way to court control.

The invert offense

The third series of the Mirror Offense is called Invert Offense. It is designed to exploit a defensive sag by the high post's defender. When it is recognized that the high post's defender is dropping off to help against the various cuts in the lane area, then the offense is instructed from the bench to run the Invert Offense. The Invert Offense has three options.

Option #1—*Both Guards Through*. The Invert Offense begins with the customary pass to O4. O2 then cuts through the lane on his give and go move, but this time he will come out ball side on the baseline about five to eight feet from the basket if he does not get the pass. O1 will always cut through the lane in this series, going either over the top of the screen, or cutting behind the screen. If O1 does not get a pass, he will stack below the O3 (Diagram 1–22). The chances are not very good that the ball can be passed to either of the cutters because of the sag of the defensive high post. Nevertheless, both cutters are coached to cut through quickly, looking for the ball to threaten the defense with penetration and encourage a defensive sag, which will help set up the next option of the Invert Offense. After the cutters have gone through and set up, O4 will look first for O2 on the baseline. If O2 is not covered, O4 should pass to the baseline and cut to the basket on a give and go maneuver (Diagram 1–23).

Option #2—*High Post Out*. This second option now gives the offense the opportunity to exploit the sag of the high post's defender on the cutting guards. O5, after screening as usual for the weakside guard, now moves toward the ball, instead of going low to screen as in the other two series. If the ball has not been passed to the baseline, it will now be passed out on top to O5. In many cases, O5 will be able to dribble into the foul circle for the open jump shot due to the sag of his defender. When this pass to O5 is made, O2 will move out to the corner, and O4 will cut to the basket which again creates a give and go situation (Diagram 1–24). If the jump shot is taken by O5, the cut of O4 puts him in good rebound position on his side of the basket, O3 will rebound in the middle, and O1 the other side of the basket. O5 is responsible for floor balance.

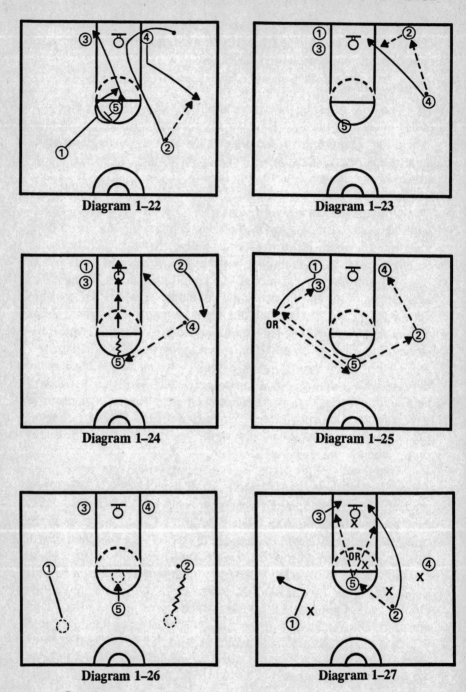

Diagram 1–22

Diagram 1–23

Diagram 1–24

Diagram 1–25

Diagram 1–26

Diagram 1–27

Option #3—*Reverse and Post*. If O5 does not have the open shot, O1 will break out of the stack. O5 will pass to O1 and he will immediately look to try and post the ball to O3. If this post set is not open, the ball is reversed to O5 again and is then passed to O2 who has moved to the wing area. O2 will then try to post the ball to O4 who has set up in the strongside low post (Diagram 1–25). This procedure of reversing the ball from side to side can be continued until the ball can be posted, or the offense can be reset (Diagram 1–26) after one attempt to post the ball on either side, and the Invert series is restarted again.

The invert offense as an automatic

The Invert Offense is also used as an automatic sequence in our offensive strategy against the man to man. Whenever the ball is passed directly to the high post from the guard position, the offense will automatically run the Invert series. The Invert as an automatic gives us a method for attacking defenses which are employing tough denial pressure on the forwards, and is also a tactic used against defenses which try to force our guards toward the middle. By using the Invert Offense in these situations, we threaten the defense with quick penetration for the easy lay up. If the penetration does not produce the shot, the remainder of the Invert Offense is then run. Diagram 1–27, shows a typical situation for automatically running the Invert Offense. O4 is being over-played effectively, so the pass is made to O5. O2 cuts hard to the basket looking for the return pass. O5 must square to the basket and read the defense, and hit the open man underneath, either O2, or O3 if his defender moves over to help on the cutting guard. O1 will not cut through in the automatic sequence; instead he moves to the wing area on his side of the floor, and if nothing is open inside O5 will pass to O1 and he will attempt to post the ball to O3. This phase of the offense is usually easy to accomplish, since O3's defender has sagged in to help against the cutting guard (Diagram 1–28). If O2 does not get open, he will exchange positions with O4 and a double post set is established on both sides of the floor (Diagram 1–29). Once again the ball can be reversed from side to side until there is an opportunity to post the ball, or the offense can be reset as previously shown in Diagram 1–26.

Variations for the mirror offense

In our offensive thinking, we are always looking for a little something extra to add, something which will fit in with what we are already

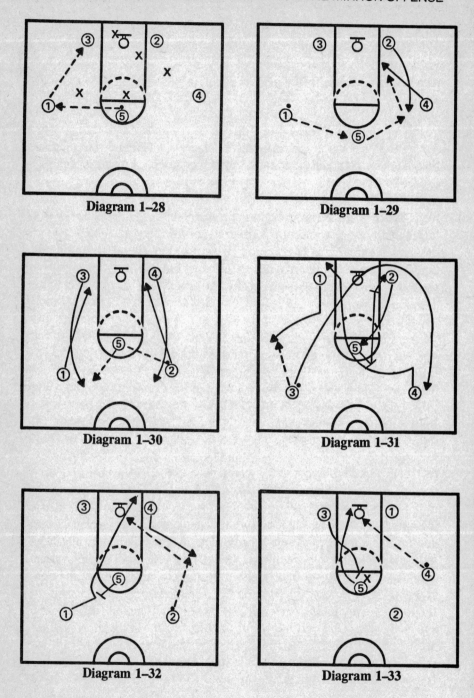

Diagram 1–28

Diagram 1–29

Diagram 1–30

Diagram 1–31

Diagram 1–32

Diagram 1–33

doing without requiring too much of a learning process, yet will provide us with the opportunity to make our offense a little more flexible. From the Mirror Offense there are three variations which can be used to provide a change of pace, and give the defense some additional problems.

INTERCHANGE

The first variation is called "Interchange." This tells the offense that the entry pass will go to the high post and the guards and forwards exchange floor positions. The ball is then passed out on top to one of the forwards, who is now a guard (Diagram 1–30), and one of the Mirror Offense series is run from this set. Diagram 1–31 shows the Regular Offense being run from the Interchange set up. This simple variation can force defenders into unaccustomed floor positions, or if the defense switches the interchange, creates the possibility of an offensive mismatch of either quickness or height.

ISOLATION

The second variation is called "Isolation." The purpose of this variation is to try and isolate a cutter in the lane for the easy lay up. The first player we try to isolate is the weakside guard, the second choice is the high post. Here is how the Isolation works. The ball is passed to O4, as usual, but O2 does not cut through the lane, instead he holds his floor position. O1 will cut behind O5 as soon as the entry pass is made, trying to catch his defender napping, since the defender has become used to O1 being the second cutter, and so might not be quite ready for this quick penetrating cut at the start of the offense (Diagram 1–32). If this option does not produce the quick basket, the cutting guard sets up in the strongside low post, and the second attempt at isolation occurs. O3 moves up the lane, as if cutting to the foul line, but instead of becoming the shooter, O3 sets a back pick on O5's defender, and O5, who is usually the screener, will break off the pick, looking for a pass from O4 (Diagram 1–33). If nothing happens with this move, the ball is passed back out on top. O4 and O1 in the low post exchange positions; O5 sets up in the weakside low post; and O3 moves to the weakside wing area (Diagram 1–34). The offense is now in the same type of set as the one which is established during the last phase of the Invert Offense, and so the ball will be moved from wing to wing until it can be posted (Diagram 1–35).

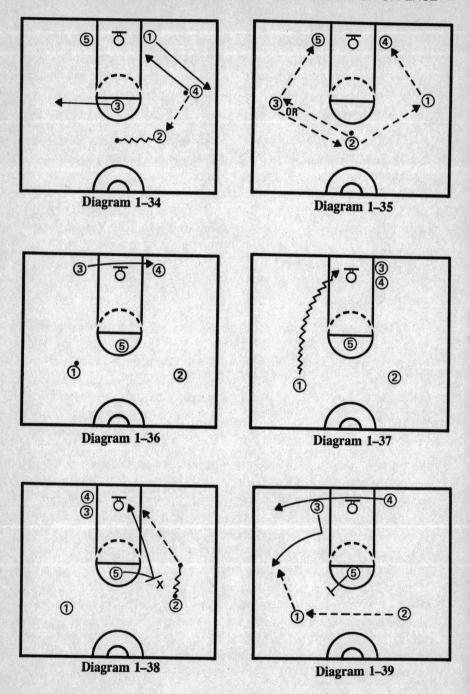

Diagram 1–34

Diagram 1–35

Diagram 1–36

Diagram 1–37

Diagram 1–38

Diagram 1–39

CLEAR OUT

The third variation for the Mirror Offense is called the "Clear Out." Our offense has three clear out maneuvers. The first is a simple one on one. A good one on one player is placed at one of the guard spots. The forward on his side of the floor clears out (Diagram 1–36), and the guard goes one on one (Diagram 1–37). The second clear out maneuver starts with the forward clearing out and then the high post and the guard on the cleared out side of the floor run a pick and roll (Diagram 1–38). The third clear out maneuver is used when we have a good leaper. We will place the player with the jumping ability at one of the guard positions and clear the side of the floor opposite the jumper. The jumper will pass to the forward on his side of the floor, and the other forward will break to the ball side corner, so that the lane area is totally cleared out (Diagram 1–39). After passing to the forward, the good jumper will break over the top of a screen set by the high post, and the forward will throw a high lob pass near the rim of the basket. The player with the good jumping ability will try to catch the ball at the top of his jump and shoot it with one motion (Diagram 1–40).

These variations are used for special situations and are called from the bench. We like them because they contain an element of surprise which can catch the defense off guard. The additional practice time spent on these variations has rewarded us with a number of key baskets during the course of a season.

This completes the description of the Mirror Offense. It has proved extremely effective against the front court man to man in all of its varieties. Although the entire package is made up of simple op-

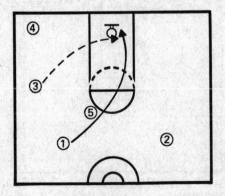

Diagram 1–40

tions, proper timing and execution are required to make the offense work. To develop proper timing and execution several drills are used. In these particular drills no defensive players are used, as the emphasis is totally on offensive execution.

Drills for the development of the mirror offense

DRILL #1 FOUR SPOT SHOOTING

1. Purpose—To develop proper shooting technique.
2. Emphasis—To improve each individual's shooting ability with instruction in regard to:
   a) Grip
   b) Shooting arm and hand alignment
   c) Sighting of the target
   d) Release
   e) Follow through
3. Procedure— (Diagram 1–41). This basic shooting drill is used daily for 10-20 minutes. The players line up in one of the four designated spots, shoot from that spot and then rotate to the next spot on their right. Each day the players are told which particular aspect of the shooting technique we want them to concentrate on, and we then expect total concentration on that fundamental for the length of the drill. Talking is discouraged unless it is of an instructional nature. The managers serve as rebounders.

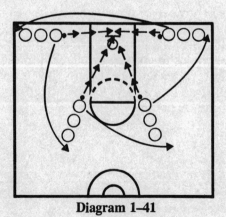

Diagram 1–41

DRILL #2 WEAKSIDE GUARD CUTS

1. Purpose—To teach proper execution of the weakside guard cuts off the high post, with proper execution of the shot after receiving a pass from the forward.

2. Emphasis—To develop the skills of:

   a) Executing a change of direction cut.

   b) Receiving a pass while cutting to the basket.

   c) Developing good body coordination for a balanced shot.

The individual points of emphasis for the cut to each of the three shooting areas depicted in Diagram 1–42 are as follows (each is described with movement being from left to right):

   a) Diagram 1–42–a—cut over the screen. The cutter moves in a straight line toward the foul circle, pushes off his left foot, rubs off the screen and breaks for the basket along the right lane line. As the cutter moves down the lane, he should carry his hands at chest level with palms toward the passer, ready to receive the basketball. After receiving the pass, the player should be conscious of lifting the right knee straight up as he goes up for the shot, so that his body will go up and not out on the lay up shot. The backboard is to be used on this shot.

   b) Diagram 1–42–b—cut behind the screen. The cutter starts his move toward the top of the key as if to break over the top of the screen. When the cutter reaches the middle of the floor, he will push off his right foot and rub off behind the screen. The same method for receiving the pass, as described above is used. However, the lay up technique is different. In this situation we want the cutter to execute a power lay up. That involves a technique in which the player comes to a complete stop on the right side of the basket, receives the pass and uses a two foot take off, and jumps straight up to shoot the lay up. Once again, the backboard is used.

   c) Diagram 1–42–c—cut to the jump shot area. The cutter begins his maneuver as if he were cutting over the top of the screen, but will continue across the top of the foul circle until he reaches the right side of the circle. Hands should be ready to receive the pass. After the pass recep-

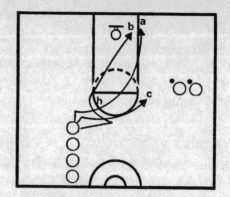

Diagram 1–42

tion, the player will pivot on his left foot, square his body to the basket, and shoot the jump shot.

3. Procedure—(Diagram 1–42). A folding chair is placed at the top of the foul circle on the left lane side of the floor, to represent the screen of the high post. A line of players is set up on the left side of the floor, and the first player in line moves into the weakside guard position. Two other players, each with a basketball, set up at the foul line extended in the strongside forward position. The first player in line in the forward area slaps the ball and the first player in the weakside guard line makes one of the designated outs, receives the pass and takes the shot. The cutter will rebound his own shot and dribble out to the passing line. The passer moves to the cutting line. Each cut is run until fifteen baskets are made, then the drill is executed on the other side of the floor, with the points of emphasis being the opposite of the ones stated above.

DRILL #3 THE VERTICAL SCREEN DRILL

1. Purpose—To develop the proper maneuvering and shooting techniques for the weakside forward in the third option of the Regular Offense and for the strongest guard in the second option of the Reverse Offense.

2. Emphasis—To teach the proper fundamentals for maneuvering and for shooting the jump shot off the vertical screen in the weakside phases of the Regular and the Reverse Offenses. These points of emphasis are:

   a) Alignment of weakside shooter on the buffer zone.

   b) Weakside shooter must wait for the high post to move down the lane and set the screen.

c) Weakside shooter will break along the lane line to the foul line. Hands should be ready to receive a pass. Catch the pass at the foul line, pivot on inside foot and square body to the basket and shoot the jump shot.

3. Procedure—(Diagram 1–43). Two players line up at the foul line extended in the strongside forward position. The first player in the line has a basketball. Another player lines up as the high post on the left side of the foul circle which approximates the high post position after screening for the weakside guard. The rest of the players line up out of bounds along the baseline on the weakside of the floor. The first player in this line moves to the buffer zone. The strongside forward slaps the ball, and the high post moves down the lane to set the screen for the weakside player. The weakside player waits for the screen, then breaks up the lane, receives the pass at the foul line, and shoots the jump shot. The screener sets up in the weakside low post and will rebound a missed shot. The passer waits until the shot is taken and then will break to the middle rebound spot. The rotation for the drill is for the shooter to move to the passing line; the passer to high post; and the high post to the end of the shooting line. After fifteen baskets are made the drill is repeated on the other side of the floor.

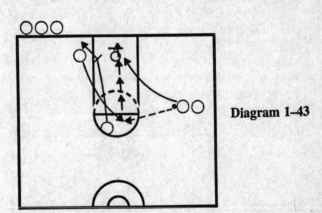

Diagram 1–43

DRILL #4 THE REVERSE OFFENSE LOW POST DRILL

1. Purpose—To develop techniques and timing for the first option of the Reverse Offense.

2. Emphasis—The skills to be developed are:

a) The development of the ability of the strongside forward to make a 90 degree cut to get open for the entry pass to start the offense. The technique is for the forward to move one or two steps up the lane, and then push off the inside foot to the foul line extended area.

b) The teaching of the weakside forward to line up on the buffer zone; wait for the screen of the guard; break either high or low off the screen; hands ready to receive the pass; and after receiving the pass shoot the hook shot, make a power lay up move, or shoot the turn around jump shot.

3. Procedure (Diagram 1–44). All the guards line up on the strongside of the floor. The first guard in line has a basketball. Two forwards take their positions, one on each buffer zone. The remaining inside players line up out of bounds along the baseline on the weakside of the floor. The strongside forward makes his 90 degree cut to get open and will receive a pass from the strongside guard. The forward then pivots toward the basket. The strongside guard cuts through the lane and sets a screen for the weakside forward. The forward breaks off the screen, receives the pass, and takes the shot. The rotation for the drill has the guard returning to the end of the guard line; the weakside forward becomes the strongside forward; and the strongside forward goes to the end of the weakside line. After fifteen baskets are made on one side of the floor the drill is flopped over to the other side.

DRILL #5 THE COMPLETE OFFENSIVE PATTERN DRILL

1. Purpose—To develop smooth execution of an entire offensive pattern by a complete offensive team.

Diagram 1–44

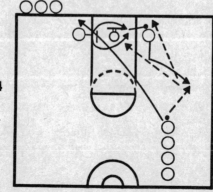

2. Emphasis—Check for proper timing of cuts and passes, and for rebounding and floor balance responsibilities in each option of the offensive pattern.

3. Procedure—This drill has two phases. The first phase is called the breakdown drill. In the breakdown drill each option is used as a scoring maneuver. A pass is made to the player who is the scoring threat in each option and this player takes his shot, and the shot must be made before the offensive sequence continues. For example, in the Regular Offense breakdown drill, the strongside guard makes the entry pass to the strongside forward and cuts through the lane on his give and go maneuver. The pass is made to the strongside guard and he takes the shot. Assuming the shot is made, everyone returns to his starting position and the offense is started again. This time the pass will be made at the second option, to the weakside guard on one of his cuts. Then the same procedure is followed through the third and fourth options, and when these options have been successfully carried out, the drill is then run on the other side of the floor. This breakdown drill teaches the players the purpose of each option of the total pattern, and gives them an understanding of what the offense is trying to accomplish, and at the same time enables the players to learn rebound and floor balance responsibilities through each option of the offense.

The second phase of this drill is called the last option drill. The players run the entire pattern through to the final option, with no passes made by the strongside forward until the final option is reached, and only at the final option will a shot occur. This drill teaches the players to move through the entire pattern quickly and smoothly and enables the total pattern to become an automatic reaction on the part of each player, and the more the pattern is a reaction the more effective it will be.

If you are going to run a multiple type of offense then this drill is a must, because it is only through this sort of drill that complete understanding and familiarity with each pattern can be achieved. This kind of drill will help replace the thinking process with a reacting process. Coaching multiple offense means that you must be willing to spend the time needed to teach the players how to carry out each pattern properly.

The value of a well executed offensive pattern is that every player knows where each of his teammates is located at any given time in the offensive pattern, and so there is less guesswork of what to do with the basketball. In addition, pattern basketball has a tendency to create team basketball because each player has a certain responsibility as each option unfolds, and these responsibilities have to be fulfilled if the pattern is to be successful. These two factors, in my opinion, are the big selling points for pattern basketball. The Mirror Offense meets these two characteristics quite well, and in addition, the minor changes of each series give it a flexibility which can take advantage of the defense. In each series of the Mirror Offense, every player has a scoring opportunity at some stage of the offense, and he is expected to take advantage of that opportunity, if he believes it is the best percentage move to make at that time. If the player doubts that it is the best percentage move, then he is expected to move the offense into its next stage, so that a better percentage situation can be achieved.

In executing the Mirror Offense, we always have our team remain in the same series until it is changed by instructions from the bench. By doing this, we avoid confusion which could arise if we attempted to run each series in sequence. For each game we establish a priority list of the order in which we will run our offenses. This priority list will depend on the style, strengths, and weaknesses of the particular opponents. This priority can change, however, during the course of the game due to something the defense might be doing, and so it is necessary to practice the entire offense each week, so that the players are prepared with all offensive weapons they have available.

The Mirror Offense was created as an attempt to solve definite problems posed by the defense. The key, then, to offensive effectiveness is that both coaches and players must become aware of how the defense is attempting to handle the various options. This recognition of the defensive strategy will enable the offense to run whichever series can best take advantage of that strategy, and the offense should then be instructed from the bench as to which series to put into operation.

The Mirror Offense can give the offensive team the initiative in the front court situation, but only if there is recognition of which series can best attack the defense. Couple this recognition with the Mirror Offense and the result will be court control.

2

EXPLOITING THE FRONT COURT
MAN TO MAN WITH
THE GUARD AROUND

TACTICAL USE OF THE GUARD AROUND

The modern game of basketball has seen more and more coaches moving to the multiple defense style of play. It is not uncommon to see a basketball team feature two or three full court presses, the same number of three quarter or half court passes, plus a variety of front court defenses. I readily agree with this concept of play because I believe that multiplicity makes for a much more interesting game for coaches and players as well as spectators. Yet many of these same multiple defense teams rely on one basic offense. A reason often given for this is that it is simply too much to expect a player to learn. I just cannot agree with that reason because if a player can learn a variety of defenses, and we all know that defense is the most demanding phase of the game to play, then how much more likely is it for the same player to learn a variety of offenses as well, because it is simply much more fun to play offense, and if it is fun the player is more apt to learn it. So I subscribe to the view that a basketball team should use a multiple offense as well as a multiple defense because I believe that the best way to be prepared for a multiple defensive team is with a multiple offensive system. With that idea in mind, I will now present a second offensive system for attacking the front court man to man, the Guard Around.

Like the Mirror Offense, the Guard Around is based on offensive movement which will produce the high percentage shot. The Guard Around threatens the defense with penetration, it creates the potential for the uncontested 15-18 foot jump shot, as well as setting up the opportunity to move the ball in to the low post. However, the manner in which these scoring opportunities are created is quite different from the Mirror Offense. In the Guard Around, only one cutter is sent through the defense. The jump shot opportunity is created for the strongside forward, whereas in the Mirror Offense the jump shot option occurred on the weakside. The low post option results when the ball is reversed to the weakside of the floor, rather than from trying to force the ball into the post from the strongside of the floor. This low post phase of the offense has proved most effective for our teams since we have rarely been blessed with big and strong inside people, and we have found that by maneuvering the offense so that the low post option occurs after the ball has changed side of the floor, we have not had much difficulty posting the ball. This low post feature is what we like best about the Guard Around, and so when we want to use more of a low post oriented attack, our team is instructed to go to the Guard Around.

The Guard Around, like the Mirror Offense, is run from the 2-1-2 offensive alignment and it has four options. However, the Guard Around is not as quick moving as the Mirror Offense; it is more of a finesse type of offensive pattern which attempts to maneuver the defense out of position and then take advantage of it. The Guard Around, then, is our change of pace offense, which presents the defense with a different look, and more importantly with a different set of problems to contend with in the front court.

THE FOUR BASIC OPTIONS OF THE GUARD AROUND

Option #1—*Weakside Guard Through*. The Guard Around is initiated with a pass to O3. O1 then follows the pass, cuts behind O3 and will get the ball back (Diagram 2–1). As soon as this pass is made to O3, O5 and O2 move to new positions. O5 clears out to the weakside low post and stacks above O4, and O2 moves to the center of the floor in line with the basket (Diagram 2–2). The first option is now set up. O3, after returning the ball to O1, breaks to the top of the key area, and sets a head hunting pick on O2's defender. O2 breaks off the screen to the basket for the potential lay up (Diagram 2–3). If a shot does occur off this option, O5 will rebound the middle, with the shooter and O4 rebounding the side areas. O3, after setting the screen, is responsible for floor balance in this option of the Guard Around pattern.

It should be noted that when O1 gets the ball back from O3 and sees the chance to drive to the basket, he is expected to take advantage of that opportunity. When O2 sees this drive taking place, he must hold up his cut so as not to take another defender into that area (Diagram 2–4).

If no shot develops from the first option, O2 sets up in the strongside low post.

Option #2—*Foul Circle Jump Shot*. If the ball cannot be passed to the cutting guard, it will now be passed to O3 in the area of the foul circle. In the majority of instances, O3's defender has a tendency to drop off his man to help out on the cut of O2, and this will enable the ball to be passed to O3 for the wide open jump shot in the foul circle. This is another example of how the uncontested jump shot will be available if it follows an option which threatens penetration of the defense (Diagram 2–5). If the jump shot is taken, O5 will again rebound in the middle, O2 and O4 rebound the sides. O3, after shooting, will move in to the long rebound area around the bottom of the foul circle, and O1 will move back out on top for floor balance.

Option #3—*Post the Ball*. When the ball is passed out on top to O3, but he is not able to get the uncontested jump shot, his responsibility is to move the ball to the weakside stack. O4 will jump out of the stack, receive the pass and immediately try to get the ball into O5. If O4 does not hesitate, he can usually get the ball inside with very little difficulty. The reason for this is that through the first and second options of the offensive pattern the two defenders on the weakside have been in a sagging situation to help out their teammates if needed, and because of their positioning they are usually unable to recover enough to keep the ball from being posted (Diagram 2–6). This is where the Guard Around pattern is valuable because it is able to take advantage

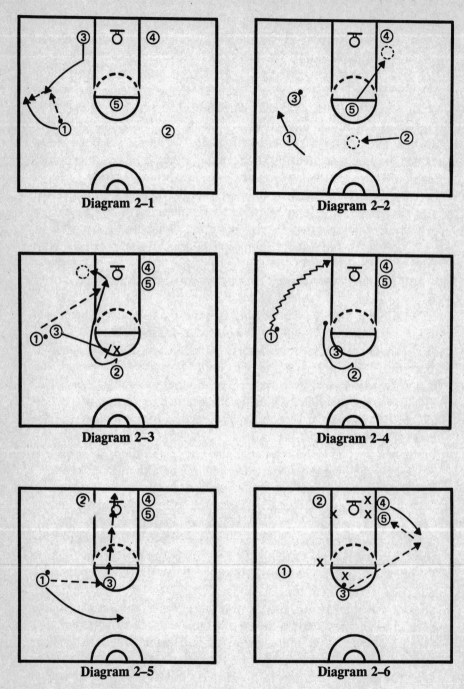

Diagram 2–1

Diagram 2–2

Diagram 2–3

Diagram 2–4

Diagram 2–5

Diagram 2–6

of the defense in this situation and finesse the ball into a high percentage scoring area.

A minor adjustment which can be made in this option is to have O5 jump out to the wing area to receive the pass from O3, and then post the ball to O4 who remains in the post (Diagram 2–7). This can be used if the forward is the better scoring threat, or as a change up from time to time.

If a shot results from this option, O2 and the shooter rebound the side areas, O3 breaks down the lane to rebound the middle area, and O1 moves out for floor balance.

Option #4—*Strongside Exchange*. If the ball cannot be posted, it is passed back out on top to O3. When this pass is made, the two players on the original strongside of the floor exchange positions. O1 will break low and set a headhunting pick for O2. O2 will wait for the pick and then break off of it to just above the foul line extended. This will usually produce the open jump shot (Diagram 2–8). Off this exchange there is always the possibility of posting the ball if there is a defensive breakdown in defending against the screen (Diagram 2–9). A shot from this option has O4 rebounding in the middle, the two players in the post areas rebounding the side areas, and O3 remaining on top for floor balance.

If no shot has occurred with the completion of the fourth option, the offense can do one of two things. They can remain in the 1-2-2 set which they have established and continue to work the ball from side to side until they are able to post the ball, or they can reset the offense (Diagram 2–10) and start the Guard Around pattern again, with the only difference being that the guards have changed sides of the floor (Diagram 2–11).

VARIATIONS FOR THE GUARD AROUND

We have used the Guard Around for about four seasons, and the more we used it, the more we liked it because of the uncommon number of high percentage shots it produced. The Guard Around did not replace the Mirror Offense, but it began to acquire equal billing in our offensive thinking. And so, as we began to add variations to the Mirror Offense to deal with particular defensive strategy, so, too, we began to add variations to the Guard Around, with the result that gradually the Guard Around has now become an entire offensive system in itself. With the following three variations, the Guard Around

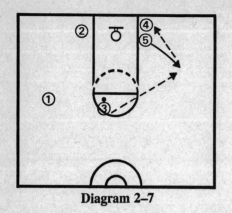

Diagram 2–7

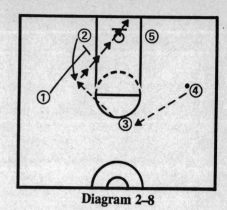

Diagram 2–8

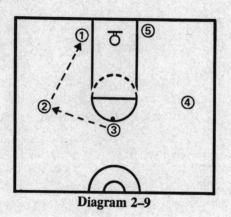

Diagram 2–9

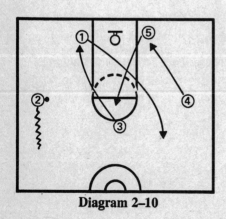

Diagram 2–10

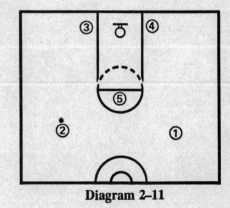

Diagram 2–11

presents a formidable weapon with which to exploit the front court man to man defense.

Bonnie cut

The first variation of the Guard Around is called the Bonnie Cut. I cannot remember where we picked up this term, probably at a clinic somewhere, but regardless of how we got this term, the Bonnie Cut refers to a special change of direction cut used by the strongside forward. O4 will run this cut after receiving a pass from O2 and give the ball back to him, as in the usual entry into the Guard Around. O4 will then break toward the top of the key as if to screen for O1. However, when O4 reaches the area of the foul circle, instead of screening, he will make a reverse pivot (i.e., he will pivot on the foot closest to the baseline, so that a forward moving from the right side of the floor would pivot on his right foot, and vice versa from the left side), which will put him in a position where he is now facing O2 who has the ball. O4 will then take a long step down the lane with his non-pivot foot, for the purpose of trying to get his defender behind him, and then slide to the low post looking for the pass from O2 (Diagram 2–12). Although the description of the Bonnie Cut makes it sound like a slow maneuver, in fact it is to be executed quickly by the strongside forward, so that the pivot, step, and slide down the lane leave the defender trailing the cutter down the lane.

The Bonnie Cut is very effective when the strongside forward's defender is trying to stay very close to his man to try and deny the pass to him after the weakside guard cuts off his screen. Once a defender has been victimized by the Bonnie Cut he will sag off his man, and the offense will have no difficulty in running the remainder of the pattern.

The Bonnie Cut can be called from the bench, but it can be used any time the forward thinks he can beat his defender with it. When the Bonnie Cut is used, O1 will remain at the top of the key, and if the ball is not posted, O4 will set up in the strongside post, and the ball will be reversed to O1 who will take the jump shot if it is open, but if it is not he will move the ball to the weakside stack side of the offense (Diagram 2–13). If no shot occurs on the weakside of the floor, the ball is reversed again as in the basic Guard Around pattern. O2 will break to the basket and set his head hunting screen, but this time it will be for O4 who made the Bonnie Cut and has remained in the strongside low

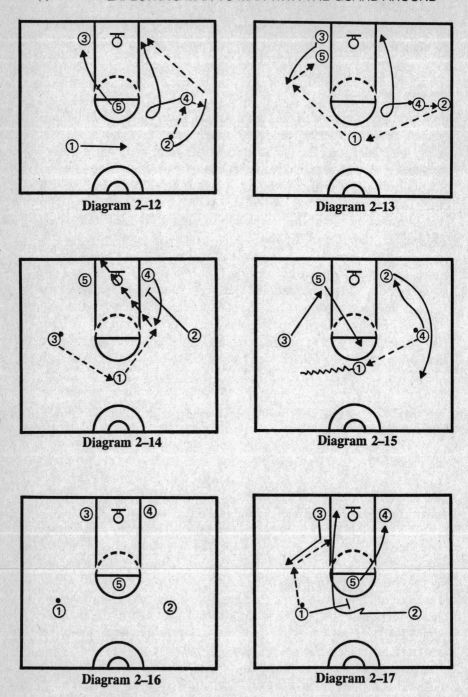

Diagram 2–12

Diagram 2–13

Diagram 2–14

Diagram 2–15

Diagram 2–16

Diagram 2–17

post (Diagram 2–14). O4 must wait on the screen, break to the wing area, near the foul line extended, and take the jump shot if it is open, or post the ball to the screener if he gets open, just as in the fourth option of the basic pattern. Again the offense can continue to reverse the ball from side to side until it can be posted, or the guard on top can dribble cut to one of the sides of the floor which signals the other players to return to their starting positions (Diagram 2–15). The offense is now reset (Diagram 2–16) and the Guard Around is started again.

Guard in

The second variation for the Guard Around is called the Guard In. This variation does not start with the usual entry of the strongside guard following his pass to the strongside forward and getting the ball back, but since the operation of the offense is basically the same Guard Around pattern it is classified with the Guard Around series. The Guard In variation was developed as a method for using the Guard Around pattern against defenses which would double team the hand off from the strongside forward back to the strongside guard to try and prevent us from effectively running our offense.

The Guard In variation is initiated with the usual entry pass to O3, but O1, instead of following his pass, breaks opposite and he sets the screen for O2, who breaks down the lane, as in the basic pattern, looking for the pass for a lay up (Diagram 2–17). After this different entry, the offensive pattern proceeds as usual. The screening O1 is now at the top of the key, and if no pass is made to O2, O1 will receive the pass and look for the jump shot, and if it is not available to him, he will move the ball to the stack side of the offense (Diagram 2–18). If the ball cannot be posted it is reversed again, and the head hunting pick and exchange takes place between O3 and O2 (Diagram 2–19). If the good percentage shot has not occurred, then once again the ball can be moved from side to side until it can be posted, or O1 at the top of the key can dribble out of the middle as a signal for the other players to return to their starting positions (Diagram 2–20), and the offense has reestablished its starting alignment, with the guards having changed sides of the floor, and the Guard Around pattern is started again (Diagram 2–21).

Wing over

The final variation of the Guard Around is called the Wing Over.

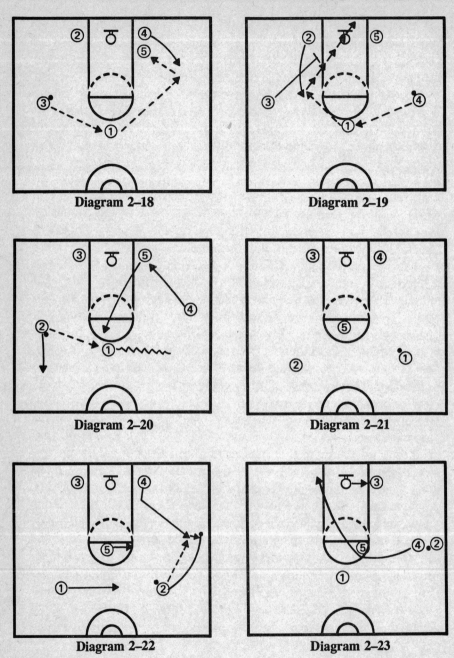

Diagram 2–18

Diagram 2–19

Diagram 2–20

Diagram 2–21

Diagram 2–22

Diagram 2–23

The purpose of this variation is to put an extraordinary amount of pressure on both low post areas at the beginning of the pattern. The Wing Over takes advantage of the defense anticipating the screening move of the strongside forward, and the clearing move of the high post to the weakside.

The Wing Over starts with the O2 and O4 hand off. O1 moves to the middle of the floor, as usual, but O5, instead of clearing out to the weakside, moves toward the basketball but remains in the foul circle (Diagram 2–22). When O4 gives the ball back to O2, he breaks toward the top of the key, as in the basic pattern, but this time, instead of screening, O4 will break over the top of O5's screen and cut to the weakside low post area. As this maneuver is taking place, O3 will move across the lane and set up in the strongside low post (Diagram 2–23). O2 must read the defense and try to get the ball into either post area, with a direct pass into the strongside post, or with a lob pass into the weakside post, depending on which defender has been maneuvered out of position (Diagram 2–24). If neither post option is available, the offense will now establish the double low post, 1-2-2 set as previously. To get into this set, the ball is moved back out on top, and O4 will break out to the wing area with O5 sliding into the post area vacated by O4 (Diagram 2–25). Now the ball is passed to O4 and he will attempt to post the ball. Once again, if no post play develops the ball is reversed and O2 will set a head hunting pick for O3 (Diagram 2–26). The reversing process can continue until the ball is posted, or when the guard on top gets the ball he can dribble out of the middle which signals the other players to return to their starting positions (Diagram 2–27) and the offensive alignment has been reestablished (Diagram 2–28), with the forwards having changed sides of the floor, and the Guard Around pattern is started again.

This completes a description of the four options of the Guard Around, as well as the variations which have been devised to take advantage of defensive reactions to the basic pattern. Like the Mirror Offense, the Guard Around can only be operated successfully if there is proper execution of the cuts and passes which comprise the offensive pattern. To develop the proper timing, a series of drills are used to teach the various parts of the Guard Around and to ensure that the players become totally familiar with the entire pattern.

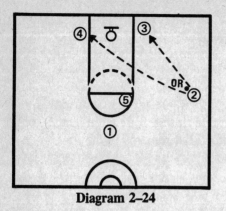

Diagram 2–24

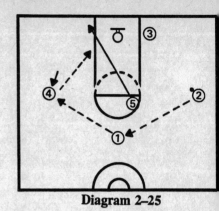

Diagram 2–25

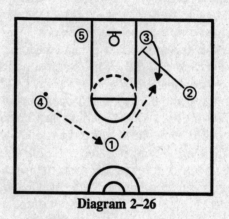

Diagram 2–26

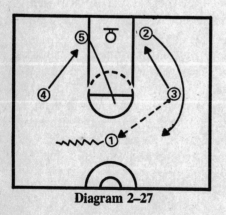

Diagram 2–27

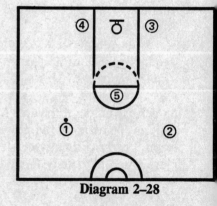

Diagram 2–28

DRILLS FOR THE DEVELOPMENT OF THE GUARD AROUND

Drill #1 guard through and jump shot drill

1. Purpose—To teach the first and second options of the Guard Around pattern.

2. Emphasis—The following three skills are to be developed:

   a) The strongside forward makes his 90 degree cut to get open, receives a pass from the strongside guard, then returns the ball to the guard who follows his pass and breaks to the top of the key area to set a screen for the weakside guard.

   b) The weakside guard should move to the middle of the floor when the entry pass is made. When the screen is set by the strongside forward, the weakside guard is to make a change of direction cut (i.e., push off the foot opposite the direction of the cut) and break down the lane to the basket. On his cut to the basket, the weakside guard should get his hands to chest level to be ready to receive the pass, and after receiving the pass he shoots the lay up using the backboard. Both the regular type of lay up, in which the cutter shoots on the move, and the power lay up, which he shoots from the two foot take off, should be practiced.

   c) The strongside forward, after screening, pushes off the foot farthest from the baseline and turns back to the area from which he came. He gets his hands to chest level, receives the pass, squares his body to the basket, and takes the jump shot.

3. Procedure—(Diagrams 2–29 and 2–30). One forward sets up the strongside buffer zone, the other forwards form a line out of bounds along the baseline. Two guards line up in the strongside guard position, the rest of the guards form a line at the weakside guard spot. An extra basketball is used in this drill. One ball is given to the strongside guard, another ball is placed on the floor in the wing area on the strongside. The strongside forward makes his move to get open, receives the pass and gives the ball back to the strongside guard. The strongside forward then moves to the top of the key area and sets a screen for the weakside guard. The weakside guard breaks off the screen, breaks down the lane and receives a pass from the strongside guard for the lay up shot. After passing to the cut-

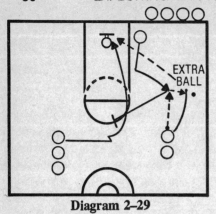

Diagram 2–29

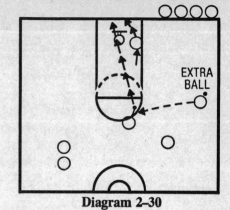

Diagram 2–30

ter, the strongside guard picks up the extra ball and passes to the strongside forward in the foul circle and the forward takes the jump shot.

The rotation for this drill has the cutter moving to the end of the strongside guard line; the strongside guard to the end of the weakside guard line; and the strongside forward to the end of the forward line. This drill is run until a total of twenty-five baskets are made; then it is switched to the other side of the floor and repeated.

Drill #2 stack drill

1. Purpose—To develop the low post phase of the Guard Around.

2. Emphasis—This drill is intended to perfect:

   a) The low man in the stack using the top man in the stack, as a screen to get open in the wing area. As the low man breaks to the wing area, the hands must be ready to receive a pass, and after the reception, that player pivots on his inside foot and faces the post man. He then must make the proper pass into the post.

   b) The post man getting his hands ready to receive a pass and working to create a passing lane. After receiving the pass, the post man is to work on the turn around jump shot, the hook shot, and the power move to the basket.

3. Procedure—(Diagram 2–31 to 2–36). The inside players line up out of bounds along the baseline. The first two in line set up in a stack along the foul lane. A coach is at the top of the key with a basketball. The low man in the stack breaks out to the

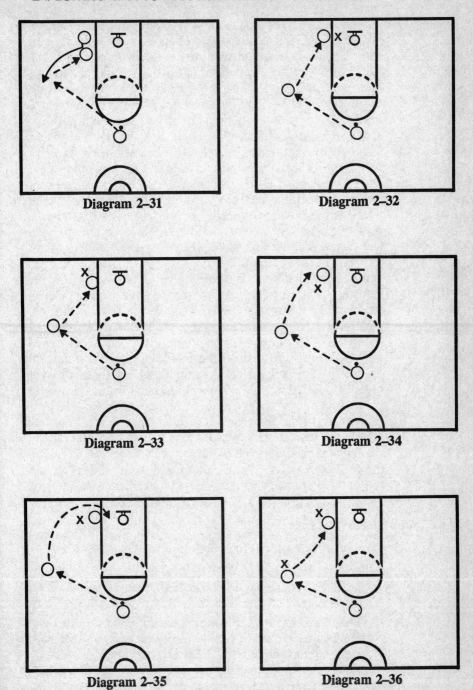

Diagram 2–31

Diagram 2–32

Diagram 2–33

Diagram 2–34

Diagram 2–35

Diagram 2–36

wing area, receives the pass and pivots to face the post man. He then passes the ball into the post and the post man takes the shot. This drill is started with no defenders (Diagram 2–31). The passer then goes to the end of the line and the shooter becomes the passer for the next player in line who becomes the post man. After working on these fundamentals so that all the inside players have had an opportunity to play both positions and have learned what is involved in the stack phase of the offense, then a third player is added to the drill to act as a defender. The drill then progresses in this fashion. First, the defender will play behind the low post man. He will not try to keep the post man from receiving the basketball (Diagram 2–32), but he will defend the offensive move to the basket. After each player has had several turns on offense, then the defender will take a three-quarter defensive position on the baseline side of the post man (Diagram 2–33). The post man must use his hands, arms, and body to create a passing lane away from the defender. Next, the defender will three quarter the post man on the high side (Diagram 2–34). Then the defender will completely front the post man and the lob pass will be practiced (Diagram 2–35). Each of these progressions should be worked on long enough so that all the inside players have several chances to play both offensive positions against these different types of post defense. The final progression for this drill is to place defenders on both offensive players, and the defenders can use any of the above tactics in defending the post. The low man in the stack must now work to get open, and after receiving the pass read the type of defensive strategy being used on the post man and then make the proper pass. The post man must work to create a passing lane and after receiving the pass make a scoring move to the basket (Diagram 2–36).

Drill #3 head hunt drill

1. Purpose—To teach the final option of the Guard Around.
2. Emphasis—The skills to be developed are:
   a) Screener must break to set screen as ball is passed out to top of key.
   b) Shooter must wait in low post area for the foul line extended, have hands ready to receive a pass, and after reception, square body to basket and take the jump shot.

3. Procedure—(Diagram 2–37). One player lines up in the weakside low post, one player at the weakside wing, and one player at the top of the key. The remainder of the players form a line in the strongside wing area, with the first player in the line having a basketball. The strongside player passes the ball to the top of the key, and as soon as this pass is released, the player at the weakside wing will break to the low post to set a head hunting screen for the player in the low post. That player will wait for the screen, then break to the wing area, receive a pass, and take his jump shot. Rotation for this drill is clockwise: shooter to passing line; screener to shooter; player at top of the key to screener; and the strongside passer to the top of the key. After fifteen baskets are made, then the drill is moved to the other side of the floor.

Drill #4 bonnie cut drill

1. Purpose—To teach the Bonnie Cut variation of the Guard Around.

2. Emphasis—The fundamentals to be developed are:

   a) The forward makes his 90 degree cut to get open.

   b) After giving ball back to guard, the forward breaks toward the top of the key. When the forward reaches the foul circle, he pivots on the foot nearest the baseline, reverses back to the ball, takes a long step with the non-pivot foot, and breaks down the lane to the basket with hands ready to receive the pass. After receiving the pass, the forward makes a scoring move.

   c) The guard who is throwing the pass should lead the cutter so that he does not have to break stride.

3. Procedure—(Diagram 2–38). This drill is set up on both sides of the floor and it alternates from side to side. A forward sets up on each side of the floor, and the remaining inside players line up along the baseline on both sides. The guards form two lines in their normal starting positions. Each guard line has a basketball. The right side of the floor begins the drill, with the entry movement for the Guard Around followed by the Bonnie Cut. As soon as the maneuver is completed, the same sequence is run on the other side. After completing their turns on one side of the floor, both guard and forward switch lines.

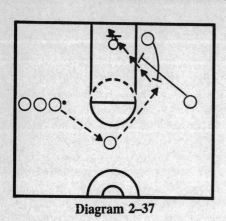

Diagram 2–37

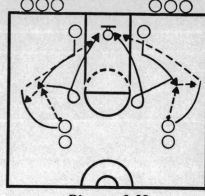

Diagram 2–38

Drill #5 wing over lob pass drill

1. Purpose—To develop the proper execution of the lob pass in the Wing Over variation of the Guard Around.

2. Emphasis—The fundamentals to be developed are:

   a) The strongside forward's 90 degree cut to get open.

   b) The strongside forward cutting over the top of the high post screen and breaking down the weakside lane line.

   c) The strongside guard developing the ability to throw a long lob pass to the weakside low post area.

   d) The strongside forward working on three offensive maneuvers: the regular lay up shot; the power lay up shot; the jumping to catch the pass and shooting the ball while still in the air.

3. Procedure—(Diagram 2–39). All guards form one line, and the first guard in the line has a basketball. One player sets up in the high post position, another player sets up in the strongside forward position. The other inside players line up along the baseline. The entry into the Guard Around pattern is made with the high post moving to the ball side of the foul circle. The forward cuts off the high post screen and breaks down the weakside of the foul lane. He will receive the lob pass from the guard and make one of his three offensive moves to score. The rotation for the drill has the guards staying in their own line, the high post goes to the end of the line on the baseline, the cutter becomes the high post. After fifteen baskets have been made the drill is run on the other side of the floor.

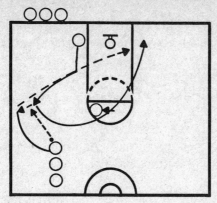

Diagram 2–39

Drill #6 complete offensive pattern drill

The purpose, emphasis, and procedure of this drill are exactly the same as described in Chapter 1 with regard to the Mirror Offense. Both the breakdown drill and the final option drill are run with the Guard Around and its variations. The breakdown drill is used to show how each option is a scoring threat and where each player belongs on the court at each option of the pattern. Then the final option drill is used to develop a smooth transition from one option to the next until the final option is reached.

Once again, it must be noted that this drill is a must if the players are to develop the total understanding necessary to run the Guard Around pattern to the peak of its effectiveness. The time spent on perfecting the operation of the Guard Around will pay offensive dividends to those who are willing to work to perfect it.

The Guard Around pattern has proved very productive over the past several seasons, and now we spend as much practice time on it as we do the Mirror Offense. I would hate to be forced to make a choice between the two offenses because I like the Mirror Offense for its quick hitting options and the Guard Around for its finesse. Each pattern complements the other.

By now, many readers may be of the opinion that the offensive systems presented in the first two chapters contain too much for a high school player to learn in the course of one season. I would be the first to agree with this opinion because in the development of our offensive thinking, neither of these patterns was totally installed in one season. We used the Regular series of the Mirror Offense, with no variations at all, for four seasons before we felt that defenses had become familiar enough with that pattern to warrant the adding of variations to the basic options. We used the Guard Around, with only the Bonnie Cut variation, for two seasons before adding anything else. So our players were carefully ingrained with just the two basic patterns before variations were added. The offensive variations of these two patterns were not added merely for the sake of change, they were added to attack defensive reactions to the basic options. And only variations were added which could be easily learned and which flowed from the basic pattern movement.

Therefore, I am not suggesting that anyone should try to install either of these entire patterns over the course of one season. I have tried to describe how these patterns evolved over the course of several seasons in a continuing attempt to improve our offensive basketball by developing a flexibility which would constantly pressure the defense.

What I am suggesting is that coaches begin to examine their own offensive system with the same intensity that they are now looking at their defensive play. Take a look at the offense and see if a minor change here or there could give a new found flexibility. Maybe one of the basic patterns described so far or a couple of the variations might fit perfectly into your present system. If they will, why not adapt them and give your players another offensive weapon to use in taking control of the front court situation.

I have found that our flexible offensive system creates a sense of offensive confidence in our players, because they have the feeling that no matter what the defense is doing, they have something, stored in their offensive bag of tricks, which will produce the good percentage shot. And the more good percentage shots the offense can get, the better their chances of scoring. This type of feeling helps develop the confidence which can make the average player good and the good player great. So I encourage coaches to develop offensive flexibility, which will give your players more confidence and enable your team to achieve court control.

3

ATTACKING THE FRONT COURT ZONE WITH THE REGULAR ZONE OFFENSE

THE REGULAR ZONE OFFENSE

On the average, our teams see the zone defense about 30% of the time during the course of a season. This does not indicate that we neglect a zone attack, for on a given night, the zone offense is going to serve as the primary front court weapon. But the fact that we see the zone defense a smaller percentage of the time means that we do not have quite as many variations in our zone offenses as we do in our man to man offenses. Nevertheless, in our zone offensive thinking, we still adhere to the concept of offensive flexibility. So our zone offenses are as flexible as we think is necessary in relation to the percentage of zone defenses we meet during the season.

The most common zone defenses used against our teams are the 2-3, the 1-2-2, and the 1-3-1. In attacking these zones, many coaches believe that it is the best policy to establish an offensive set which is the opposite of the defensive set. For example, attack an even front zone (e.g., 2-3) with an odd front offensive set (e.g., 1-3-1 or 1-2-2), and attack the odd front zone (e.g., 1-2-2 or 1-3-1) with an even front offensive set (e.g., 2-1-2 or 2-3). This strategy is fundamentally sound because it always enables the offense to establish a formation from which the seams of the zone can be attacked. The seams of the zone are vulnerable because they represent those gray areas separating one zone from the other, and attacking those spots often may lead to confusion of responsibilities on the part of the defenders which can then be exploited by the offense.

I agree that this is good, sound strategy, and in our zone offenses we have the capability of attacking with either a one or two man front, but I also believe that there are other offensive principles to be followed which are more important than the alignment of players. These principles represent the basic offensive philosophy we use in attacking any type of front court zone. These general guidelines are as follows:

1. *Movement*—The offense must have a planned pattern of movement of both players and basketball to create problems for the defense. An offense which simply stands around against the zone will be ineffective.

2. *Penetration*—The first objective of our offense is to penetrate the zone, to move the ball inside the defense. If penetration can be achieved, a high percentage shot will follow. The zone defense can often give the impression of being a very strong defense on the perimeter of the floor, but if an effort is made to penetrate inside that defensive perimeter, a defensive breakdown will occur and the good shot will be produced.

3. *Overload*—As our zone offense is moving through its various phases of attack, the purposeful movement of the players is such that an overload, or outnumbering offensive situation will be set up. The purpose of the overload movement is to place more offensive players in certain areas of the court than there are defenders available. One of our basic zone offenses is based totally on this sort of overload principle, and will be completely covered in Chapter 4, but regardless of which zone offense is being executed there will be player movement on either the strongside or the weakside of the floor to create an overload, and then take advantage of that situation to secure

the high percentage scoring opportunity.

4. *Reverse the Ball*—The zone defense is always concerned with the location of the basketball, and as the ball moves, the defense will overshift with it. Therefore, if the defense has been able to deny the good shot on one side of the floor, the offense must be able to reverse the basketball to the weakside of the floor in an attempt to obtain the high percentage shot before the defense can completely readjust itself. The zone offense must be set up so that it has the capacity to swing the ball from side to side until the zone breaks down and then the offense must take advantage of the breakdown.

5. *Patience*—Attacking the zone requires, most of all, a patient attitude on the part of the players. Against the zone, the offense will seldom get the quick, spectacular movement which produces the wide open shot. Instead, the offensive players must be taught to read the defense to see what the defense is trying to take away and then attack what the defense is giving up. If the zone is working hard to deny penetration, the offense must look for penetration, but if it is not available, don't force it, and instead reverse the ball and get the good shot somewhere else. If, on the other hand, the defense tries to stop the reverse of the basketball, then the offense must look for the opportunity to penetrate. It simply boils down to the premise that the offense must learn to be patient enough to probe the zone defense for weaknesses and then exploit them. If patience is not a priority in the front court zone offense, then the offense is playing into the defense's hands and letting them control the front court situation instead of the offense calling the shots. Patience will give the offense control of the situation.

With these guidelines as a basic foundation, our zone offenses are further divided into a strongside phase and a weakside phase. Then, because of our belief in the value of offensive flexibility, the zone offenses will have several variations. The first of our zone offenses is called the Regular Zone Offense, and as with the majority of our offensive patterns, it is run from the basic 2-1-2 set.

STRONGSIDE PHASE OF THE OFFENSE

The Regular Zone Offense starts with a pass to the strongside forward. An important coaching point on this entry pass is that the forward should receive the pass below the foul line extended (Diagram 3–1). The reason for this floor location is to put the maximum amount of pressure on the inside zone defenders, for if the ball is below the foul line extended it is nearly impossible for the defenders on top of the zone to cover it. As this pass is made, the offensive guards will exchange positions to try and attract the attention of the top defenders and keep them from sagging into the middle (Diagram 3–2). The guard moving to the strongside of the floor will move to a position which will enable him to receive a pass from the strongside forward without defensive pressure. The guard moving to the weakside will set up in a position near the foul circle about halfway between the top of the key and the foul line. With these opening entry moves completed, the offense is now ready to attack the zone defense. The strongside attack will go through three phases in its attempt to penetrate the defense.

> 1st Phase—*High Post Roll Low*—The first attempt at penetration is made by O5. As the ball is passed to O4, O5 rolls down the lane on the ball side, looking for the pass, and sets up in the strongside low post (Diagram 3–3). If the defense does not deny this pass O4 is expected to post the ball and let O5 make a move to the basket. As this pass is made, O4 will move several steps toward the basket, and if the defense collapses on the low post area, the ball can be passed back out to the forward for the standing still jump shot. If O5 takes his shot, O4 will break into the middle to rebound, with O3 and O5 rebounding on the sides. O2 who moved weakside will move to the long rebound area in the middle and O1 who moved strongside will be responsible for floor balance.

> 2nd Phase—*Weakside Flash*—If the ball cannot be posted, a second attempt at penetration is now tried. This second attempt is carried out by O3. As O5 rolls down the lane, O3 looks for an open spot in the high post area, and if a pass is not made to O5 as he rolls, O3 breaks to the open spot, looking for the pass (Diagram 3–4). If the pass is made to the flashing O3, he is to square to the basket, and if he is left open he is to take the uncontested jump shot. If the jump shot is taken, O4 will rebound the middle, O5 and O2 will rebound the side areas, the shooter will rebound the long rebound area in the middle and O1 will have floor balance. If the pass is made to the flashing O3 but as he squares to the basket he does not have the uncontested jump shot, he must read the defense and put the third phase of the strongside offense into operation.

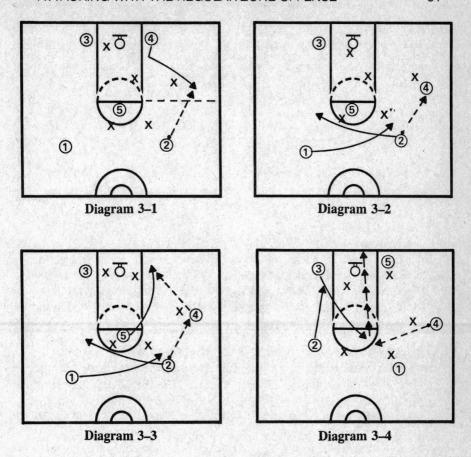

Diagram 3–1   Diagram 3–2

Diagram 3–3   Diagram 3–4

3rd Phase—*Front Door, Back Door*—As the pass was made to the flashing O3, O2 on the weakside of the floor has moved into the weakside low post area, so that a double low post set has been established. If no shot is available to the forward he looks inside to see if he can post the ball. If a defender has moved toward him from the strongside of the floor then he should be able to pass the ball to O5 who set up in the strongside low post (Diagram 3–5). This option is referred to as a pass to the front door, since it is occurring on the same side of the floor. However, if the defender has moved to cover the flashing O3 from the weakside of the floor, then O2 who has broken to the weakside low post should be open, and O3 should be able to make this pass which will set up a backdoor type of play and should produce the lay up shot (Dia-

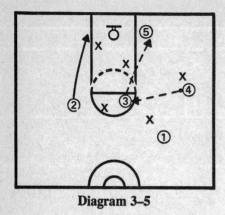
Diagram 3–5

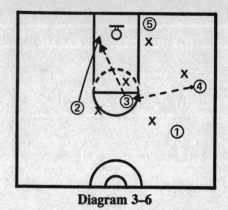
Diagram 3–6

gram 3–6). If neither of the penetrating passes can be made, the ball is passed back out either to O4 or to O1 and if the uncontested jump shot is available it should be taken, with the rebounding and floor balance responsibilities the same as described in the second phase of the offense.

These are the three attempts at penetration which make up the strongside phase of the Regular Zone Offense. The strongside forward must control the situation. When he receives the entry pass it is his responsibility to square toward the basket and read and then react to the defensive play. If the defense sags off the strongside forward and gives him the 15-18 foot jump shot, then he should take it. If he does not have this shot, he must then read the roll of the high post and post the ball if it is open. If the high post roll is covered, the strongside forward then looks for the flashing weakside forward and will pass the ball into the high post area if it is open. If the strongside forward is unable to penetrate the defense with a pass to either the low or high post areas, he will then pass the ball back out to the strongside guard, and this pass will now move the offense into its Reverse Phase.

REVERSE PHASE OF THE OFFENSE

As the basketball is passed back out to the strongside guard, it now becomes that player's responsibility to read the defense, and that read will determine whether the strongside guard will put the Reverse Phase into its first phase, or bypass the first phase and start the second phase.

1st Phase—*Penetration to Foul Circle*—When O1 gets the ball from O4, he is instructed to take a look at what the top of the zone defense is doing. If the top portion of the defense splits, with one defender taking the ball and another defender moving to deny a pass to O2, then O1 should be able to penetrate the defense with a pass to O3 who flashed to the high post and has remained there as the Reverse Phase of the offense begins (Diagram 3–7). If this pass is made, then the offense is in the same situation as in the second and third phases of the strongside offense, and O3 will react in the same way, by either taking the uncontested jump shot from the foul line or by using the front door, back door, sequence (Diagram 3–8). If this penetrating pass does not produce a shot, then the ball goes back out to O1 and he will move the offense into the second phase. In order for the second phase to start after the penetrating sequence has not produced, it will be necessary for O2, who had broken to the weakside low post, to return to his position near the foul circle. If this penetrating pass cannot be made to begin with, because of the sag of the weakside of the defense into the foul circle area, then O1 will bypass this phase of the offense and start the second phase.

2nd Phase—*Weakside Jump Shot*—If the defense at the top of the zone is denying a pass into the high post area, the ball is then passed to O2 near the foul circle. If O2 has the standing still jump shot he should take it (Diagram 3–9).

3rd Phase—*Post the Ball*—When O2 receives the pass, but the defense is able to recover and deny the open shot, he is instructed to then look to the low post area on his side of the floor, because O5, who rolled to the strongside post at the start of the offense, will cut across the lane and set up in the ball side low post (Diagram 3–10). Since this move occurs behind the inside defenders, it is often possible for the pass to go inside, and the high percentage shot results.

4th Phase—*Corner and Roll*—If the low post area is not open for a pass from O2, then O5 will clear the area and move 12-15 feet toward the corner, and as the post is cleared, O3, who flashed to the high post and has held his position there, will now roll down the lane to the low post (Diagram 3–11). O2 reads the defense and gets the ball to the open man. The player in the corner may have the open jump shot, or as he moves to the corner he may be covered by a defender which means the pass could be made directly to the player rolling down the lane. Another possibility is

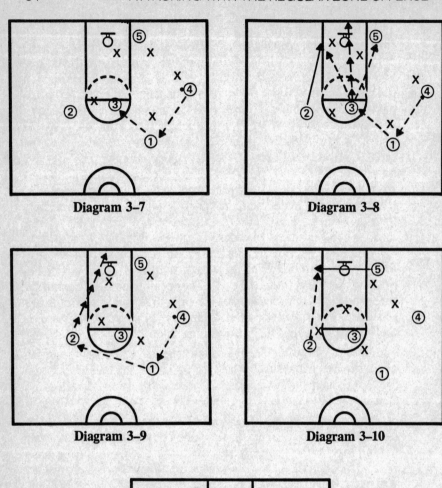

Diagram 3–7

Diagram 3–8

Diagram 3–9

Diagram 3–10

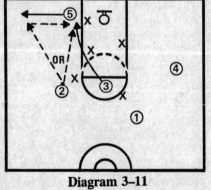

Diagram 3–11

that if the ball is passed to the corner but the open shot is not there, the ball can be passed from the corner into the low post. Again it is a matter of reading the defense and taking advantage of what is available to the offense.

If a shot is taken in the 2nd, 3rd, or 4th phases of the weakside offense, the rebounding and floor balance responsibilities remain constant. O5 is always responsible for the ball side rebound area, the flashing O3 is always responsible for the middle, O4 rebounds the side area away from the ball, the guard on the ball side rebounds in the foul circle area, and the guard away from the ball is responsible for floor balance.

In most situations a good shot will have been produced before the final phase of the weakside offense has been reached. However, in the event that a good shot has not occurred by the time the entire pattern has been carried out, the Regular Zone Offense does have a continuity to it to keep the pattern moving. If nothing has developed by the time the Corner and Roll phase has occurred, then the ball will be reversed to the other side of the floor from guard to guard and then to the original strongside forward. The two players involved in the Corner and Roll phase will now move to new positions. The player who ended up in the low post will move across the lane to the ball side post, and the player who ended up in the corner will flash to the high post (Diagram 3–12). If penetration is achieved, then the weakside guard will break to the weakside post as usual. If no penetrating pass is made then the Corner and Roll move is repeated (Diagram 3–13). By continuing to reverse the ball, this flashing and then the Corner and Roll phase can continue until penetration is achieved. In most cases, however, a good shot will be available before much of a continuity has to be run.

This Regular Zone Offense has been used successfully against all varieties of front court zones. The key to its success is the players' learning to read the defensive pattern, to take advantage of penetrating when possible, to reverse the ball when penetration is not possible. The players must be taught to strive for the close to the basket shot as the first priority, and the standing still jump shot as the second priority. The players will learn that the good shot will eventually result if they will be patient enough to move through the pattern until the defense breaks down.

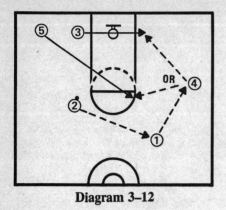
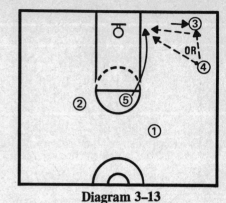

Diagram 3–12   Diagram 3–13

VARIATIONS FOR THE REGULAR ZONE OFFENSE

There are two variations for the Regular Zone Offense, which give the defense a different look, but do not change the objectives of the offense. The first variation is called "Opposite," and it operates from the 2-1-2 set. The second variation is called 1-3-1, and operates from a different offensive set.

Opposite

In the Opposite variation, when the ball is passed to O3, O5 will roll down the lane away from the basketball and sets up in the weakside low post. O4 will flash as in the Regular Zone Offense, but in this case he has the entire lane area to maneuver in to find an open spot. The guards cross as usual (Diagram 3–14). If O4 gets the pass, he squares to the basket and reads the situation. If he has the open shot he should take it. If he gets defensive pressure from the weakside he should try to get the ball to O5 who is now in the weakside low post (Diagram 3–15). If a shot occurs from this penetration, O5 will rebound on the weakside, O4 will rebound in the middle, O3 his side of the floor, O1 on the weakside has the long rebound area in the middle, and O2 on the strongside has floor balance. If no shot is available the ball is passed back out to O3 and he will reverse the ball to the other side of the floor. This reverse sequence will also develop if no penetrating pass is made. The objective of this reversing of the ball is to try and get a pass into the weakside low post before the defense can deny it (Diagram 3–16). If nothing develops, then the offense is reset with O5 moving back to

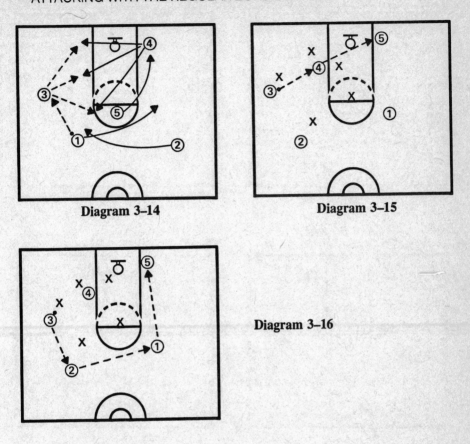

Diagram 3–14   Diagram 3–15

Diagram 3–16

his original position, and O4 returning to his starting spot (Diagram 3–17). Then the Opposite sequence would be run again. On some occasions when the zone is sagging into the middle a great deal to deny the flash from the weakside, the high post will be open for a cross court lob pass from the strongside forward (Diagram 3–18). This has been a relatively safe pass for us in the past, and we expect the strongside forward to use it when a particular type of defensive strategy makes it available.

1-3-1

The second variation is the 1-3-1 which will operate on the same principles for attacking the zone, but provides us with a different look.

If the entry pass is made away from the low post, O3, O5 will

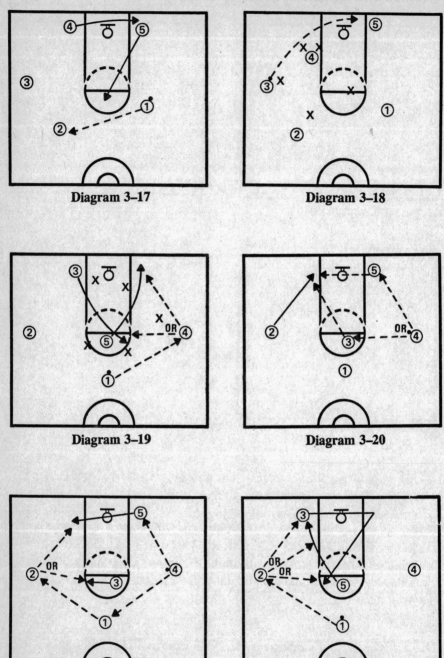

Diagram 3–17

Diagram 3–18

Diagram 3–19

Diagram 3–20

Diagram 3–21

Diagram 3–22

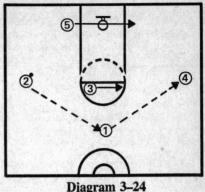

Diagram 3-23   **Diagram 3-24**

immediately roll down the ball side lane looking for the pass, and O3 will flash high (Diagram 3–19). O4 will read the defense as usual and attempt to make a penetrating pass if it is available. If the ball is passed into either the low or high post areas, O2 will break to the weakside post as a potential pass receiver or rebounder (Diagram 3–20). This is the penetration phase of the 1-3-1, and if no penetration occurs, the ball will be reversed to the other side of the floor, with the two post players following the ball (Diagram 3–21). If a pass is made into the post, then the wing man away from the ball will break low as previously described. This procedure of reversing the ball and the post men can then continue until penetration can be achieved or the open jump shot is available.

If the entry pass is made to O2 on O3's side of the floor, the first option for O2 is to post the ball immediately. If this pass cannot be made, then O3 will clear out and O5 will roll low, and then O3 will flash to the high post (Diagram 3–22). As previously described, if a pass is made to either post area, O4 breaks to the weakside low post as a potential pass receiver or rebounder (Diagram 3–23). If no shot develops, then the ball is reversed, and the two post men follow the ball as before (Diagram 3–24). This reversing sequence can then be continued until penetration is achieved or the open jump shot can be taken.

These two variations are all that we have found to be necessary to add some flexibility to the Regular Zone Offense to make it as difficult as possible to defend. The various movements of the offense create situations which cause the defense to move, but the player positioning is such that no matter how the defense moves, something is always available to the offense. The offensive players, however, must learn to read defensive maneuvers, and make the proper choice of the available options. To try and teach our players the ability to recognize and make the proper choice, we use a series of drills.

DRILLS TO DEVELOP THE REGULAR ZONE OFFENSE

Drill #1 guard exchange drill

1. Purpose—To develop the proper guard movement and positioning at the start of the Regular Zone Offense and to practice reversing the basketball to the weakside guard for the jump shot.

2. Emphasis—To perfect the following techniques:

   a) Strongside guard starts offense with a pass to the strongside forward, then he crosses in front of the weakside guard and establishes a position near the weakside foul circle, halfway between the top of the key and the foul line.

   b) Weakside guard crosses behind strongside guard to the strongside of the floor and establishes a position in line with the strongside forward. The guard then gets hands to chest level to be ready to receive a pass from the forward, and upon reception, he passes to the guard at the weakside of the foul circle.

   c) After the strongside guard has moved to the weakside, he gets hands ready to receive the basketball, and upon reception, he squares to the basket and takes the jump shot.

3. Procedure—(Diagram 3–25). A manager or a coach acts as the strongside forward. One guard sets up in the strongside guard spot with a basketball, the remainder of the guards form a line on the weakside of the floor. The strongside guard passes to the strongside forward and he and the weakside guard exchange positions. The forward holds the ball for about a three second count then passes out to the guard who has crossed to the strongside of the floor. This guard then reverses the ball to the guard who has moved to the weakside of the floor for his jump shot. The rotation for the drill has the shooter moving to the end of the weakside guard line, and the weakside guard becomes the strongside guard. When fifteen baskets are made on one side of the floor. the drill is then used on the other side of the floor.

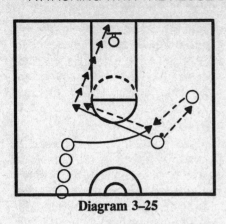

Diagram 3-25

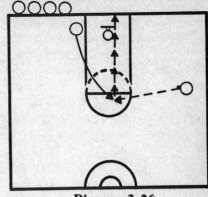

Diagram 3-26

Drill #2 penetration drill

1. Purpose—The Penetration Drill has two basic purposes:

    a) To develop the timing of the flash cut by the weakside forward to the high post.

    b) To develop the ability of the flashing forward, after receiving the pass, to read the defense and make the proper decision as to whether he should take the jump shot or find the open man underneath the basket and pass to him.

2. Emphasis—Weakside forward will break to the foul circle with hands ready to receive a pass, and after the reception will square to the basket and make the proper choice whether to shoot or to pass underneath, depending on the defensive reaction.

3. Procedure—The Penetration Drill is practiced in three stages.

    1st Stage—(Diagram 3–26). One forward takes the position of strongside forward with the basketball. One forward lines up on the buffer zone on the weakside of the floor. The remaining forwards form a line, out of bounds, along the baseline on the weakside. The weakside forward flashes to the high post area, receives a pass from the strongside forward, squares to the basket and takes the jump shot. The rotation is from shooter to passer, from passer to end of line. After fifteen shots are made on one side of the floor, the drill is run on the other side.

    2nd Stage—The drill sets up in the same fashion but a

player is added in the high post. The strongside forward slaps the basketball and this signals the high post to roll low and set up in the strongside low post. As the high post clears out, the weakside forward flashes to the foul circle, receives the pass from the strongside forward, squares to the basket, and passes to the player in the low post for a power lay up (Diagram 3–27).

After this sequence has been carried out to the coach's satisfaction, a defender is then placed in the lane area. The drill is run again, and the pass is made to the flashing weakside forward. The defender does not try to deny this pass, but after the pass is made, the defender makes a definite move to play defense either against the man in the low post or against the man in the high post. The flashing forward must now read this defender and make the proper choice, either the jump shot (Diagram 3–28), or the pass to the low post for the power lay up (Diagram 3–29). The same three offensive players will run through this drill several times before they are replaced. The defense is told to mix up the coverage to keep the offense guessing, so that a definite reading process will be developed.

3rd Stage—The next step is to add a line of guards to the drill. The first guard in line will set up in the position he would be in after exchanging at the start of the Regular Zone Offense. The strongside forward slaps the basketball, the high post rolls low, and the weakside forward flashes to the foul circle and receives the pass. As the pass is made, the weakside guard will break to the weakside low post. The flashing forward, after receiving the pass, will square to the basket and pass the ball to the weakside guard for a power lay up (Diagram 3–30). As with the other stage of this drill, this phase is practiced until the coach is satisfied with the timing, then two defenders are added. These defenders do not deny the pass to the flashing forward, but after he has received the pass, they will play defense on any two of the players involved in the drill, which will now force the flashing forward to read the defense and then make the proper choice. The choices available to the flashing forward, depending on the defensive play, will be either the jump shot (Diagram 3–31), or the pass to the original high post

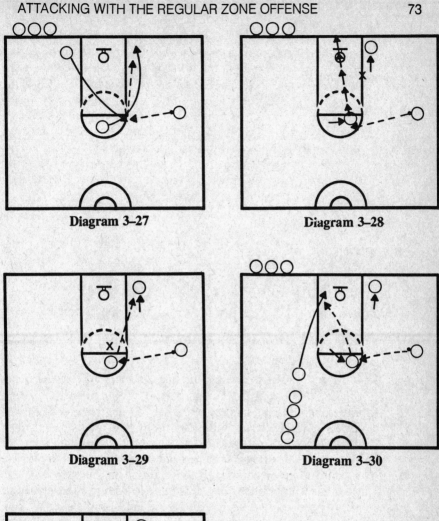

Diagram 3–27

Diagram 3–28

Diagram 3–29

Diagram 3–30

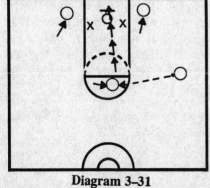

Diagram 3–31

player who rolled to the strongside low post at the start of the offense (Diagram 3–32), or the pass to the weakside guard who broke to the weakside low post, when the pass was made to the flashing forward (Diagram 3–33). The defenders are instructed to definitely take away two of the three options available to the three options flashing forward, so that one choice is always there, and it is up to the forward to read the right choice he should make. The three players on offense should repeat this drill several times with the defense mixing up their coverage so that different choices will have to be made.

Drill #3 reverse phase drill

1. Purpose—To develop the ability of the guard who has moved to the strongside at the start of the Regular Zone Offense, to read the defense and to make the proper pass in starting the Reverse Phase of the Regular Zone Offense.

2. Emphasis—The guard on the strongside must establish a passing lane for the strongside forward, get hands up, ready to receive the pass, then read the defense at the top of the zone and make the proper pass.

3. Procedure—One player sets up in the strongside forward position with a basketball. Two guards set up in the positions they will be in after exchanging at the start of the Regular Zone Offense. One player sets up in the high post area, the position that the weakside forward will occupy after flashing. Two defenders are also used. One defender will play the strongside guard, the other defender will set up on the weakside of the floor, and he will choose which area to cover, either the high post area or the weakside guard area. The strongside forward will reverse the ball to the strongside guard, and he will read the defense. If the weakside defender covers the weakside guard area, then the strongside guard will pass the ball to the player located in the high post for the jump shot (Diagram 3–34). If the weakside defender sags into the middle to deny the pass to the high post, then the strongside guard will reverse the ball to the weakside guard for the jump shot (Diagram 3–35). The same players will run through the drill several times before they are replaced.

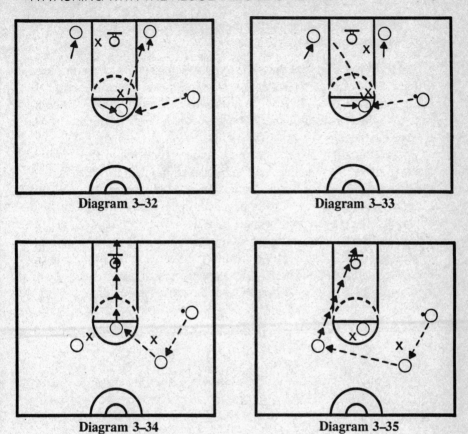

Diagram 3-32   Diagram 3-33

Diagram 3-34   Diagram 3-35

Drill #4 complete offensive pattern drill

This drill is run as previously described in the first and second chapters. The breakdown phase is used first, with the ball being passed to the player carrying out each option, and the shot is taken. Then the final option phase is used with the offense going through its movement, but no shot occurring until the last option is reached. As mentioned before, we think that this drill is a most important one in building an understanding of the offense, and so we consider it a must if we are to be successful in using a flexible type of offense. This Complete Offensive Pattern Drill is used not only for the basic Regular Zone Offense, but for the variations as well, so that there is total understanding concerning the operation of the offense on the part of the players. Anything less will negate the value of flexibility.

These four drills are the only ones used to install the Regular Zone Offense. The final step is to work the offense on a five against five half court situation. The five on five work will enable the offense to combine both the Penetration and Reverse phases as a total offense against the various zone defenses.

The strength of the zone defense is many times more a psychological one than a physical one, and so by demanding that the players read the defense, be patient in their attack, keep probing with both ball and player movement, the zone's psychological value will be broken down, and the players will become confident that they have the necessary tools to attain the high percentage shot. Obviously, the more high percentage shots a team can get against the zone, the better the chance for defeating the zone. The Regular Zone Offense has been that kind of an offense, and as a result it has enabled us to establish court control.

4

DOMINATING THE FRONT
COURT ZONE WITH
THE OVERLOAD OFFENSE

THE OVERLOAD OFFENSE

The Overload Offense is our second basic means for attacking the front court zone defense. It is designed to take advantage of the player with the good outside shooting ability. The offense operates in such a fashion that the more the defense becomes concerned about stopping the outside threat, the more they leave themselves vulnerable to penetration. This offense can be run so that the outstanding shooter can always be maneuvered so that he is the primary scoring threat. If you are fortunate to have two great outside scoring threats, then the offense can be run so that either can threaten the defense, but the beauty of the Overload is that you need only one real good outside shooter to make this offense work.

The Overload Offense has been used successfully against the 2-3, the 1-2-2, and 1-3-1, and the 3-2 zones. The basic theory of this offense is to maneuver the best outside shooter into either corner by the help of a screen, then get the ball to him in the corner and if he is left open let him fire away. As the defense begins to try and take away this scoring threat, they will leave themselves open to be exploited by the other phases of the Overload Offense.

As with the Regular Zone Offense, the Overload follows our basic principles for attacking the front court zone defense. The Overload will have movement of both players and the basketball. There will be opportunities to penetrate inside the zone. There will be a phase for reversing the basketball to the other side of the floor, if nothing develops on the overload side. Making the Overload Offense work will, once again, demand reading, maneuvering, and patience on the part of the offensive players, and when these qualities are present the Overload Offense becomes a devastating weapon which will bring about domination of the front court zone.

METHODS OF ACHIEVING THE OVERLOAD

The usual alignment for the Overload Offense is the basic 2-1-2 set. We also run the Overload Offense from a 1-2-2 set, but that is one of the variations and will be discussed later in the chapter. The Overload Offense can be set up in one of three ways. The first method is to position the best shooter in the high post, and then let him break into either corner off a screen by one of the forwards (Diagram 4–1). A second method is to have either guard take the overload position. This is done with a lateral pass to the weakside guard followed by a cut through the zone to either corner (Diagram 4–2). If this method is used the high post player will move out to the vacated guard position because if the cutter decides to overload on the same side he came from, the remaining guard would have a very difficult pass to get the ball into the opposite corner, so the high post moves out so that the ball could be moved into the corner a little easier (Diagram 4–3). The third method for maneuvering into the overload is to have one of the forwards clear to the opposite corner off the other forward's screen. If this method is used then the player in the high post will fill the spot vacated by the forward so that the offense will have a player in position to rebound on the weakside, which is a most important rebounding position when shots are taken from the corner (Diagram 4–4).

Any of these three methods can be used to achieve the overload set. It might be a question of personnel or simply a matter of personal

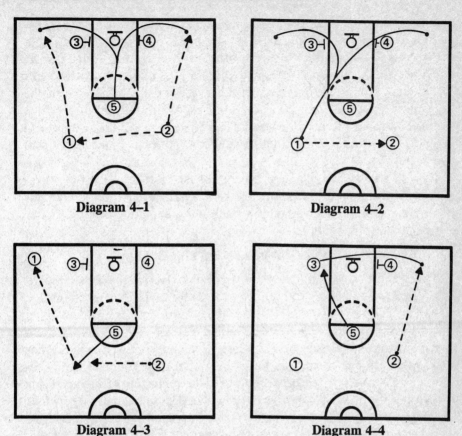

Diagram 4–1

Diagram 4–2

Diagram 4–3

Diagram 4–4

preference. We have used the first method exclusively for the past two seasons and have been well pleased with the results. However, if your best outside shooter is a guard, as was the case with one of our teams, this necessitates moving one of the forwards out on top to play one of the guard spots. This was no problem for us, but it could be a problem if the inside people were not capable of playing that far away from the basket. In that case, one of the overload methods should be used. If the best outside shooter is a forward, it is a relatively simple matter to place him in the high post and put the usual high post player in one of the forward spots.

Like the Regular Zone Offense, the Overload Offense is divided into two phases. In the Overload Offense these two phases are the Overload Phase and the Reverse Phase. The first phase threatens the defense with the talent of the good outside shooter, but has other potential scoring options available if the defense becomes too concerned with stopping the threat from the corner. If the defense does take away the scoring opportunity of the Overload phase, then there is a Reverse Phase to move the ball to the other side of the floor and produce a high percentage shot before the overshifted defense can recover to stop it. The two phases of the Overload Offense give it a balance which can produce scoring opportunities on either side of the floor which makes it a most effective offense against a defense which will try to overshift and deny one phase of the attack. This strategy by the defense will enable the offense to exploit the overshift and come up with the high percentage shot.

There are also three variations for the Overload Offense, which give it the desired flexibility. Two of the variations are very minor adjustments, the third variation is based on running the offense from a different front court set.

OVERLOAD PHASE OF THE OFFENSE

The first scoring situation which the Overload Offense tries to create is the standing still jump shot from the corner by a good outside shooter. To set this possibility up, the Overloader, O5, will cut down the lane and break below either forward (i.e., on the baseline side). O4 must make a definite effort to screen the defender closest to the corner so that O5 can break free to the corner, receive the pass from O2, square himself to the basket and take the jump shot (Diagram 4–5). This is the primary objective and if a shot does result the offensive set is such that excellent rebound coverage is assured by the positioning of the two forwards, and in addition, if the shot is taken from the corner, O1 will break down the lane and rebound in the middle. O2 will be responsible for floor balance. Another method that we have successfully used in regard to offensive rebounding when one of our forwards has been placed in the guard spot, because one of the guards had become the Overloader, was that on a shot we would always send the forward out on top to the middle rebound spot, and the other guard would always be responsible for floor balance.

After the Overload Offense has produced several good shots from the corner, and if the corner shooter has hit a few in a row, the defense will now begin to realize that the player cutting to the corner is a primary scoring threat and they will realize that a concerted effort must be made to defend against this maneuver. As the defense becomes overly concerned with the player overloading in the corner, they will leave themselves vulnerable to other areas of attack.

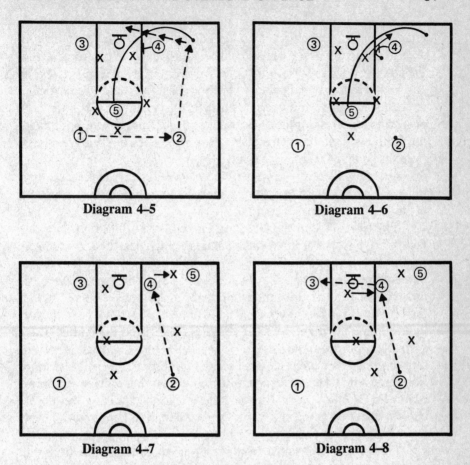

Diagram 4–5

Diagram 4–6

Diagram 4–7

Diagram 4–8

The first possibility occurs when one of the bottom defenders tries to move as quickly as possible over the forward's screen to try and deny the pass to the corner, or if this is not possible, at least get to the corner in time to deny the uncontested jump shot. When this defensive maneuver occurs, the screening forward, O4, is coached to make his definite screening effort, facing the defender as usual, but when the defender frees himself from the screen, will turn toward the foul circle (Diagram 4–6) and expect a penetrating pass from O2 (Diagram 4–7). O2 must also be aware of what the defense is doing and be ready to make this pass when it is available. This pass will usually produce the easy inside shot either right away, or if the inside defender's overshift, O4 can dump the ball off to O3 who will be open (Diagram 4–8).

A second method of getting the ball into the low post is possible after the ball has reached the corner but the defender has been able to slide to the corner as the pass is being made, to prevent O5 from having the contested shot. When this defensive maneuver takes place, O5 is coached to look immediately into the low post area, and if the post man is open, the ball is to be passed inside (Diagram 4–9). O4 in the low post, who screened for the Overloader as the offense began, has turned toward the ball as described above, and if he does not receive a pass from O2, continues to turn toward the corner, so that he is still facing the ball. If O4 receives the pass from O5 he will either make a scoring move, or if the weakside defense overshifts to stop him, dump the ball off to O3 as previously described.

The final stage of the Overload Phase of the offense involves the possibility of penetrating with the ball to the high post area. As soon as the basketball is passed into the corner to O5, O1 is coached to move into the area of the foul circle, find an open spot, and set up there. If nothing has developed from the overload situation, then the offense is instructed to look for the opportunity to move the ball into the high post area to O1. This movement can develop either from the corner (Diagram 4–10), or from the low post (Diagram 4–11). If the ball is passed into the high post area the offense will now have a 3 on 2 situation which must be taken advantage of quickly, before the defense can recover. So O1 has the job of reading the defense and making the proper choice, either his jump shot from the foul line, or a pass to whichever low post player is open.

If no shot has resulted from the Overload situation, or from the pass to the high post area, then the ball is passed back to O2 and the offense now moves into its Reverse Phase.

REVERSE PHASE OF THE OVERLOAD OFFENSE

When O2 recognizes that no shot will develop from the Overload Phase of the offense, he is instructed to create a passing lane so that he can receive the basketball and initiate the Reverse Phase of the offense. As soon as the pass is made from the Overloader to O2, O1 will move back out to his starting position (Diagram 4–12), so that he can receive a pass from O2 and move the ball to the weakside of the floor. When the pass is made to O1, O3 moves out to the wing area to receive a pass, and O4 breaks across the lane to the low post on the ball side

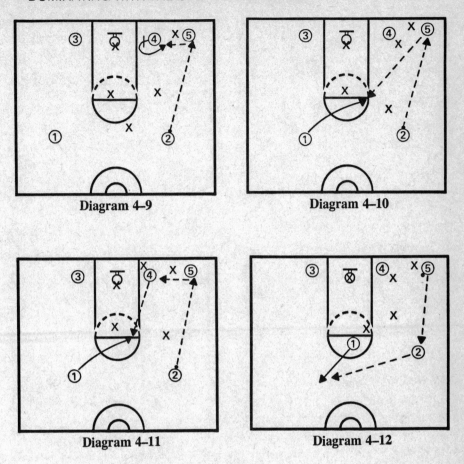

Diagram 4–9

Diagram 4–10

Diagram 4–11

Diagram 4–12

(Diagram 4–13). This is an effective sequence against the defense which has overshifted against the Overload Phase of the offense, because it enables the offense to move the ball into the low post before the defense can recover and deny the entry. As the pass is being made to the weakside wing area, O5 will move into the low post on his side of the floor, O2, who is now on the weakside will circle in behind the top of the defense to the foul line area for the possible penetrating pass (Diagram 4–14). If a shot occurs from these offensive moves then the two players who are set up in the low post positions will rebound the side areas, O2 in the foul circle will rebound in the middle, and O3 who passed the ball will rebound in the middle, and O3 who passed the ball will break for the long rebound area in the middle. O1 left on top

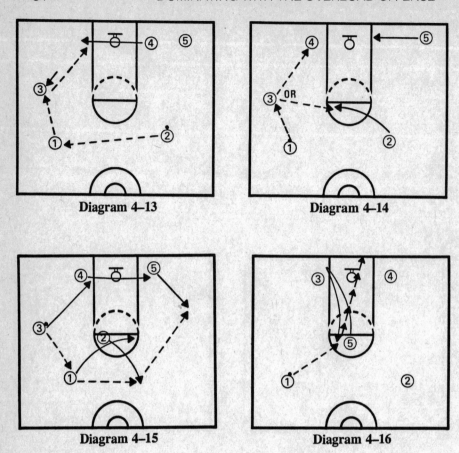

Diagram 4–13

Diagram 4–14

Diagram 4–15

Diagram 4–16

will be responsible for floor balance. If no shot is produced with the Reverse Phase, then the ball is reversed again to the other side of the floor, and the same offensive sequence is used again with the player who was the Overloader breaking out to the wing area, the other two inside players filling the post positions, while the weakside guard again breaks to the foul circle (Diagram 4–15). This sequence can then be continued until a high percentage shot is produced.

VARIATIONS FOR THE OVERLOAD

The Overload Offense is given added effectiveness by the addition of three variations which create the element of flexibility which prevents the defense from being able to completely anticipate what is going to occur everytime the Overload pattern is started. Two of these variations are very minor adjustments within the basic pattern. The third variation is the Overload pattern run from a different offensive set and in a different sequence.

Fake overload

The first variation is called "fake overload." After the defense has seen the basic Overload pattern run through several sequences, they will begin to anticipate the Overloader's move to the corner. When this defensive anticipation begins, a very simple, but very effective adjustment is the fake overload. In this variation, the Overloader will start down the lane as in the usual overload move, but when he reaches the low post area, instead of continuing into the corner, he will break back up to the foul line (Diagram 4–16). This move will usually produce the wide open jump shot for your best shooter. If this move fails to produce the shot, then the offense is started over again and the basic overload pattern is run. This variation can also be run if the Overloader does not start from the high post. If the Overloader is one of the guards, then he will make his cut through the lane, to the low post, and then pop back out to the foul line which will be open because the high post player will have moved out to fill a guard spot (Diagram 4–17). If the ball cannot be passed into the high post area, then the guard will break down the lane again and overload in one of the corners and the offense continues as usual. If the forwards are the Overloaders, then this variation is run with one of the forwards breaking across the lane and when reaching the low post cutting to the foul line, which will again be open because the high post man will have cleared out to the low post (Diagram 4–18). Once again, if no pass is made into the high post, then the player in the high post will then complete his overload cut by moving back down the lane and into one of the corners, and the offense will continue as usual. The fake overload can be run by the Overloader on his own, when he feels that the defense is over-anticipating, or it can be called from the bench.

Low post adjustment

The second variation is called the "low post adjustment." The low post adjustment is a maneuver used to try and achieve penetration of the ball into the low post. The variation works in this way. After the ball is passed to O5 in the corner, he looks into the low post area. If O4

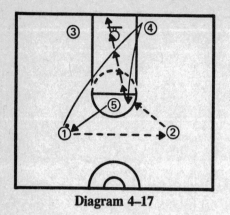

Diagram 4–17

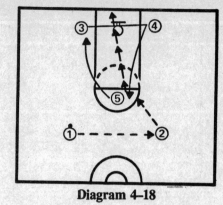

Diagram 4–18

is covered, he will slide up the lane toward the foul line, and O3 will break across the lane to the strongside low post area (Diagram 4–19). In most instances the inside defense will not be able to cover the entire lane area, and so it is a matter of the Overloader getting the ball to whichever forward is open. When the overload low post adjustment is used, O1 will not break into the foul circle, but instead remain in his original position. However, if the ball is passed inside, O1 will break to the weakside low post area where he will be in position for either a backdoor pass or for weakside rebounding (Diagram 4–20). If the ball is not passed into the post areas, then it is reversed. O3 will break back across the lane to the wing area on the ball side, and O4 who moved up the lane, will break across to the low post on the ball side. O5 will move in to the weakside low post and O2 will break to the foul circle (Diagram 4–21). The Reverse Phase of the offense will now be carried out as previously described. The low post adjustment is called from the bench and is used primarily when we are interested in definitely getting the ball inside.

1-2-2 offensive set

The third variation for the Overload Offense is the running of the offense from a 1-2-2 offensive set. In the offensive pattern, the wing men are the overloaders and the low post men are the flashers and screeners. The point man is simply responsible for getting the offense started, reversing the ball, and maintaining floor balance. In the 1-2-2 variation an attempt to penetrate the defense is made first, and if this is not successful, then the overload phase follows. The 1-2-2 variation

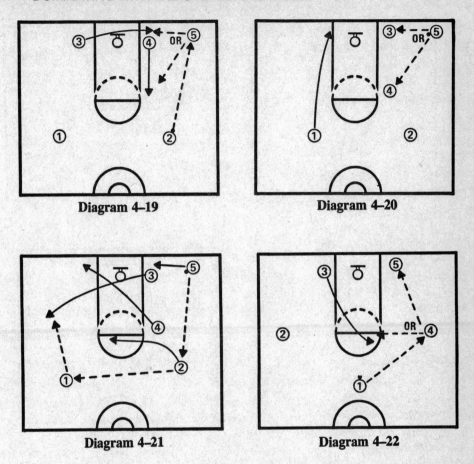

Diagram 4–19

Diagram 4–20

Diagram 4–21

Diagram 4–22

begins with a pass to one of the wings. When this entry pass is made, the weakside low post, O3, will flash to the foul circle (Diagram 4–22). The strongside wing, O4, looks to pass the ball to O5 first, O3 second. If either pass is made, then O2 will break to the weakside low post to be in position for either a backdoor pass or for rebounding on the weakside of the floor (Diagram 4–23). If no pass is made, O2 holds his position. If a shot is taken in this stage of the offense O2 and O5 rebound the sides of the basket, O3 will rebound the middle, O4 will rebound the long rebound area in the middle, and the point man will stay back for floor balance. If no penetrating pass is made, or no shot results, then the ball is reversed and now the overload phase of the offense occurs. O4 will pass the ball back out on top, and after making

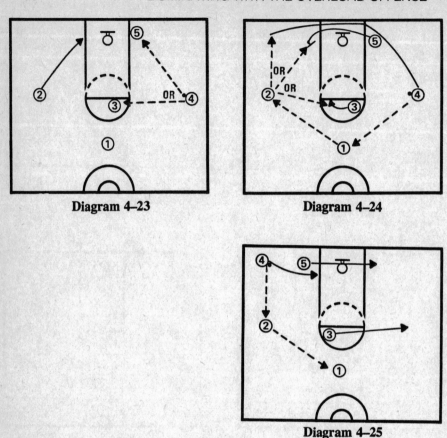

Diagram 4–23

Diagram 4–24

Diagram 4–25

this pass, O4 and O5 will clear to the opposite side of the floor. O5 will establish a screen on the lane line around the buffer zone and O4 will break on the baseline side of the screen and move to the corner. O3, who flashed high at the start of the offense, will remain in the foul circle area and follow the ball as it moves around the perimeter of the offense. When the ball is moved to the wing area on the original weakside of the floor, O2 will read the defense and depending on its reaction, he will move the ball to either the corner, the low post, or the high post (Diagram 4–24). If a shot is taken in this phase of the offense, O3 in the high post will always rebound the weakside, even if he is the shooter. The screener, O5, will rebound the middle, O4 who cut to the corner will rebound the area on the side of the basket, and O2 who passed the ball will take the long rebound position in the middle. The point

man, once again, is responsible for floor balance. If no shot develops
through these two stages of the offense, the ball is passed back out to
the point man, O3 in the high post moves to the open wing area, O5 in
the low post changes to the other side of the floor, and O4 in the corner
moves into the low post on his side of the floor (Diagram 4–25). The
1-2-2 set has now been reestablished and the offense will be started
again.

This concludes the description of the basic pattern and the variations which comprise the Overload Offense. It is an effective attack
against the front court zone defense because it challenges the defense
to try and stop the good shooter from obtaining the open shots and
gunning them down from outside. But at the same time, if the defense
becomes too concerned with one offensive player, then other offensive
maneuvers can be used to secure the high percentage shot and so the
offense contains all the necessary weapons to ultimately dominate the
front court zone defense.

However, the Overload Offense, like the Regular Zone Offense,
depends for its success on the capability of the offensive players understanding what is expected of them to make the offense work. The Overload Offense, just as every other phase of our offensive attack, requires
players who can learn to read the defense, maneuver into proper positions on the floor, and patiently move both themselves and the basketball until the high percentage scoring opportunity is made available.
Then the players must seize that opportunity.

These characteristics are not developed simply by talking about
them, by diagrams on a chalk board, or by handing out play books. All
of these methods may be a help in the total understanding of the offense, but primarily the players have to learn by doing. The players
must be exposed to situations in which they are confronted by having
to make the proper choice of what to do with the basketball, for it is
only through exposing them to these types of decision making ac-
tivities that they can truly learn what is involved in the pattern. Therefore, as with the other front court offenses, the Overload Offense is put
together with a series of drills which develop the various phases of the
offense.

DRILLS TO DEVELOP THE OVERLOAD OFFENSE

Four drills are used to install the Overload Offense. In the first
three drills, defenders are used to force the offensive players to read
defensive coverage and then make the proper choice.

Drill #1 basic overload drill

1. Purpose—To develop the movements and timing of the overload phase of the Overload Offense.

2. Emphasis—
   a) Overloader cuts to corner on the baseline side of the screen; has hands ready to receive a pass from the strongside guard; and if the pass is made he squares to the basket and will take the jump shot if it is uncontested, but if the defender has moved out to contest the shot, the Overloader will pass the ball inside to the low post.

   b) Screener sets up screen by facing the defender, then, after screening, turns toward the basketball with hands ready to receive a pass from the strongside guard. If pass is made to the corner, the screen will continue to turn toward the ball and face the Overloader with hands ready to receive a pass from the corner. If pass is made into the low post, the low post player will take the ball to the basket with some type of scoring maneuver.

   c) Passer, who is set up in the strongside guard position, will read the defensive coverage, and then pass the ball to the open man.

3. Procedure—The Basic Overload Drill has two stages.

   1st Stage—Offensive players are positioned in the high post, the strongside low post, and the strongside guard spot. The strongside guard has a basketball. One defender is stationed in the lane area, and he is instructed to do one of three things, either cover the low post man or try to deny the pass into the corner or move out to the corner quickly after the pass has been made and deny the jump shot. The rest of the inside players form a line along the baseline, the remainder of the guards form a line behind the strongside guard.

   The strongside guard will slap the ball and this signals the Overloader to break down the lane, cut on the baseline side of the screen and move to the corner. If the defender stays with the post man, the strongside guard will pass the ball to the corner and the Overloader will take his open jump shot (Diagram 4–26). If the defender tries to deny the pass to the corner, then the strongside guard will pass inside to the low post man (Diagram 4–27). Finally, if the defender takes the post man, but then moves out to defend against the jump shot, then the Overloader will pass the ball into the low post (Diagram 4–28).

The defender will remain in the drill for several turns and will mix up his coverage. The rotation of the offensive players has the guards simply moving from passer to the end of the line, the Overloader becomes the screener, the screener goes to the end of the line, and the next player in line becomes the Overloader.

If this basic overload move is going to occur from

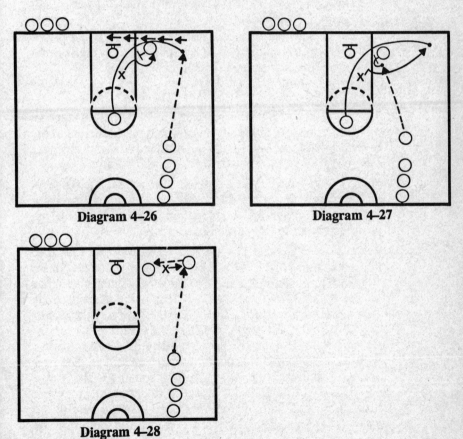

Diagram 4–26

Diagram 4–27

Diagram 4–28

another floor position, either the guard or forward area, then this drill is run exactly as described with the only adjustment being the starting position of the Overloader.

2nd Stage—For the next part of the Basic Overload Drill, another offensive player is added, and he will set up in the weakside low post. Another defender is also placed in the lane area. The drill is then run as described above, with the strongside guard reading the defensive coverage and passing to the open man. The purpose of the offensive in the weakside low post is that he is available for a pass from the strongside low post if the weakside defender moves over to the strongside (Diagram 4–29). The two defenders will again remain in the drill for several turns and vary the defensive coverage. The strongside guards rotate through the guard line, and the inside offensive players rotate from weakside low post to high post to strongside low post to the end of the line.

Drill #2 foul circle drill

1. Purpose—To develop that part of the Overload offense in which the weakside guard maneuvers into the foul circle area, receives a pass, then reads the defense and makes the proper offensive play.

2. Emphasis—Weakside guard will circle into the foul circle area from the weakside of the floor, gets hands ready to receive a pass from the corner, and after receiving the pass, square to the basket and react to the defensive coverage.

3. Procedure—Offensive players are set up in both low post spots, one corner, and in the weakside guard area away from the offensive player in the corner. The player in the corner has the basketball. Two defenders are placed in the lane area. The other inside players form a line along the baseline, the rest of the guards form a line on the weakside of the floor. The offensive player in the corner slaps the basketball, and this signals the weakside guard to maneuver into the foul circle. The pass is made to the weakside guard, and he squares to the basket and reacts to the defensive coverage with either the jump shot if both post men are covered (Diagram 4–30), a pass to the weakside low post (Diagram 4–31), or a pass to the strongside low post (Diagram 4–32). Defenders remain in drill for several turns. The guards rotate through the guard line and the inside

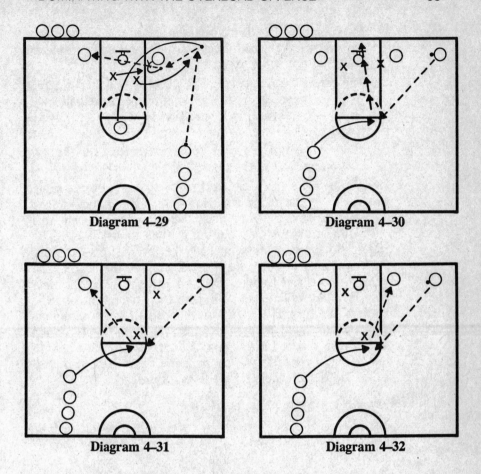

Diagram 4–29   Diagram 4–30

Diagram 4–31   Diagram 4–32

players rotate from weakside post to strongside post to the corner to the end of the line.

Drill #3 overload reverse drill

1. Purpose—To develop the timing and offensive maneuvers required in carrying out the Reverse Phase of the Overload Offense.

2. Emphasis—

   a) Weakside post makes a quick angle cut to just below the foul line extended, with hands ready to receive the pass. After receiving the pass from the weakside guard, he squares to the basket, reads the defense and makes the proper choice.

b) Strongside post makes a quick move across the lane and fills the spot vacated by the weakside post and gets hands ready to receive the basketball.

c) The original strongside guard who has now become the weakside guard with the reversing of the basketball, will break into the foul circle area and be ready to receive a pass.

d) The offensive player in the corner will move in to the low post on his side of the floor.

3. Procedure—The Overload Reverse Drill is set up the same way as drill #2, with the exception that the guard line is on the overloaded side of the floor, and either a coach or manager sets up as the original weakside guard, with a basketball. The coach or manager slaps the ball and the post man on his side of the floor breaks out for the pass, squares to the basket, and reads the defensive reaction to the offensive moves of the other players. The two defenders will take away two of the possible choices, so the player with the basketball must recognize which choice is the proper one, either the jump shot (Diagram 4–33), or a pass to the low post (Diagram 4–34), or a pass to the high post (Diagram 4–35). Rotation is the same as in drill #2, with the defenders taking several turns.

Drill #4 complete offensive pattern drill

The development of our various front court offenses would not be complete without the running of the Complete Offensive Pattern Drill, and so we use this drill for the Overload Offense, just as we

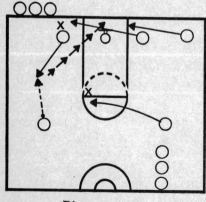

Diagram 4–33

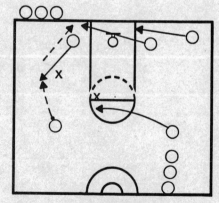

Diagram 4–34

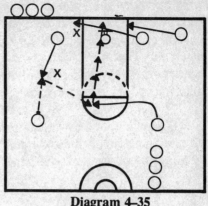

Diagram 4–35

do for our other patterns. The drill is run with the breakdown phase where each possible option is used as a scoring maneuver, and then the total pattern is run with the last possible option serving as the scoring maneuver. This drill enables the players to see how the entire pattern flows from one phase to the other, so that a total understanding of the pattern is developed.

The Overload Offense has proved to be a very good partner with the Regular Zone Offense in the attempt to defeat the zone defense. Whereas the Regular Zone Offense is a more balanced style of attack, the Overload is geared toward letting the outstanding outside shooter gun the zone down. The value of the Overload is that it assures you of an effective zone attack even if you have only one good shooter on the team because this is the one offense designed to take advantage of the good shooter's talent. But regardless of how many good outside shooters a team may have, the Overload is a worthwhile variation to the Regular Zone Offense because it gives the defense a different look, causes them to become spread out in trying to keep the offense from getting the open shot, and this means that when the defense is concerned with covering a lot of floor area, the possibility for penetration inside the defense is increased.

We have found that the term "overload" is not only an accurate description of the offensive alignment and pattern, but it also accurately describes what happens to the zone defense when it is confronted by this offensive pattern. The zone defense becomes overloaded trying to defend itself, and the more it attempts to adjust to the offensive pattern, the more vulnerable it becomes. In time the confidence of the zone defense is destroyed, because they have seen the good shooter get wide open shots from either corner, and in trying to prevent this they have been victimized by the movement of the basketball inside the zone for the high percentage shots. The offense is now in control of things, and is on its way to total domination of the front court situation.

So if the zone defense has proved troublesome to your offense at times, why not put an overload pattern in your attack and watch your offense short circuit the zone defense. This will give your offensive system another weapon with which you can establish court control.

5

PRODUCING DECISIVE RESULTS WITH THE SIDELINE FAST BREAK

THEORY OF THE SIDELINE FAST BREAK

If an offensive system is to be totally flexible, then it must include a fast break phase in its offensive arsenal. The fast break gives the offense the threat of the quick score, the threat of the sudden spurt of baskets which can bring about the turning point in a game and put your team in control of the situation. The fast break has the potential for attacking the defense with an offensive thrust before the defense has had time to regroup and get set, which then gives the offense an obvious advantage in its struggle to defeat the defense.

However, I further believe that the only kind of fast break style which can do these things consistently is the style which is based on discipline and is under control at all times. The fast break system must be based on certain principles which will serve as a guide to the attacking players, it must be organized in such a manner and developed through certain types of drills which will help the players learn to make the judgment of when to take the fast break and when to set up in a front court offense.

I enjoy watching the fast break in action when it is kept under control, but I detest the fast break when it becomes merely a baseline to baseline, race horse style of play. The reason that I oppose the race horse fast break is that I believe that the fast break contains within it its own element of self destruction. By that I mean that if the fast break gets out of control, it can produce so many turnover situations with your team spread out so much all over the floor that all of a sudden the fast break backfires and begins to produce easy baskets for your opponents. Therefore, I want my basketball team to be able to employ the fast break and employ it with as much skill as they can possibly develop, but I also want them to be in total control of the fast break when they are employing it, so that it does not backfire.

These two factors, the fast break with control, and the elimination of unnecessary turnovers, are the two primary reasons why I believe in the sideline fast break. By sideline fast break I mean that the basic theory is to advance the basketball rapidly into the front court after securing the rebound, or picking up a loose ball, but the route of advance is along the sideline. Although the basketball is moved up court along the sideline, the purpose of that movement is the same as the ordinary, down the middle type of break. We are trying to create an offensive situation in which the offensive players move down the floor quickly enough so that they outnumber the defense which will most often result in the high percentage shot for the offense.

I am well aware of the fact that the majority of the fast breaking teams subscribe to the theory that the fast break cannot work successfully unless the ball is moved to the middle of the floor by the time it reaches half court and then advanced down the middle to the foul line. This method obviously creates the setup for a balanced attack against the defense, since the offense can attack to either side. It is hard to argue against that idea, and I also like to see the basketball moved to the middle, but only after it has been advanced into the front court, and not before. My reasoning is this, think back to fast break situations which your team has been involved in, and I am sure that you can recall many occasions when your team has secured the rebound, thrown the perfect outlet pass, gotten the ball beautifully into the middle of the floor, and as the ball is dribbled into the front court, a defensive player comes up behind the dribbler and bats the ball out of his hands, and stops the fast break. Or, once again the good outlet pass is made, but the defense is able to deny the pass to the middle and so the break is stopped before it had a chance to get started. The point that I am trying to make is that it is a natural tendency of defensive players, as well as a common coaching point, to retreat back to the basket they are defending by moving down the middle of the floor when the ball changes hands so that they can set up a defensive perimeter around the area of the foul circle. Therefore, I would rather give up the theory of balancing the court with the ball in the middle of the floor, if it means attacking into the strength of the defense, and instead, for the sake of better protection of the basketball while it is being advanced, move it along the sideline where there will be little, if any, defensive pressure encountered.

Beside the mere fact that the sideline affords a safer line of advance with the basketball, we have also observed that it is a tendency of the defending players not to move as far out on the floor to stop the basketball when it is on the side. This means that the offense is able to move closer to the basket with the basketball, usually within 8-10 feet, before meeting defensive pressure, which obviously increases the scoring opportunity for the offense. When, on the other hand, the basketball is in the middle of the floor, the defenders will attempt to stop it somewhere near the top of the foul circle, which will be some 18 feet from the basket. So by advancing the ball into the scoring area by means of the sideline, the offense will gain some 8-10 feet of floor space, and the closer the offense can get to the basket, the higher its percentage of completing a successful fast break.

With the basketball on the side, the ball handler also has a better picture of what is happening. When the ball handler squares to the basket, he will be lined up at approximately a 45 degree angle to the basket. This angle permits him to use his peripheral vision to see what is going on in most of the front court, an advantage the ball handler in the middle of the floor does not have, unless he turns his head. This advantage gives the ball handler on the side the opportunity to see both the defensive and offensive movements which are developing. This gives the ball handler an overview of the situation which gives him the necessary information so that he can make an accurate judgment as to whether it is to the advantage of the offense to continue the fast break, or whether it would be more advisable to hold the break up and set up in a front court offense.

Thus in our experiences with the sideline fast break we have found, that although we give up balancing the court by advancing the ball along the sideline, we gain an element of safety, which cuts down on unneccessary turnovers, we gain the opportunity of getting the ball closer to the basket before encountering defensive pressure, which increases the chances of scoring, and we gain the concept of control because of the ball handler's ability to see the front court situation as it develops. These factors combine to create a fast break which offers the offense the best chance of achieving success because it is founded on a theory of discipline and control, and as such, the sideline fast break tends to eliminate the haphazard advance of the basketball, where the only concern is to get the shot off and little attention is paid as to whether the break should be held up and a front court offense established.

Basketball players like to execute the fast break. The fast break is exciting, it is crowd pleasing, and it is fun, and the more enjoyable the game is for the players, the more effort they will exert. But when the basketball players get caught up in the fast break, they sometimes tend to lose all perspective and get completely out of control because of the nature of the game. So, if the fast break is to be a part of your offensive system, then I believe that it is to your own best interest to build a fast break in which the elements of control can override the players' tendency to get involved in a baseline to baseline contest. In my experience, the sideline fast break is the answer to this problem.

Fastbreak principles

In organizing the fast break, the first thing done is to divide the court lengthwise into three lanes, the middle lane, and two wing lanes (Diagram 5–1). After dividing the court in this manner, the next step is to establish a set of principles which the sideline fast break will be built on. These basic principles are as follows:

1.   The defensive rebounder is to outlet the basketball in one of the wing lanes, usually the wing lane on the same side as the ball is rebounded. The outlet area in the wing lanes extends

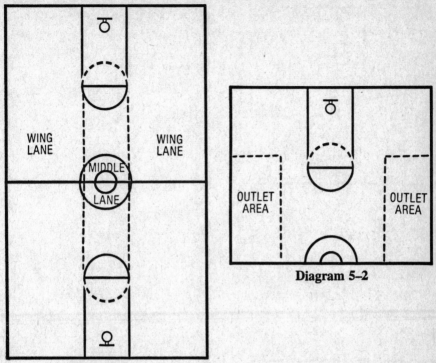

Diagram 5–1

from just below the foul line extended to the half court line (Diagram 5–2). This large outlet area is established so that the outlet man has room to maneuver to get away from defensive pressure.

2. The player who receives a pass in the outlet area is coached to pivot upcourt after receiving the outlet pass and read the defense before starting to dribble. This technique is used first of all so that the outlet man does not fall into the habit of beginning to dribble immediately upon reception of the outlet pass and possibly charging into a defensive player who has moved in front of the outlet man and established his defensive position. The second reason for this pivot and read technique is that the outlet man's rule is that when looking upcourt, if he sees a teammate ahead of him, and in the same wing lane, he is to pass the ball ahead, up the floor. If no teammate is ahead of the outlet man, he is to dribble the ball up the sideline.

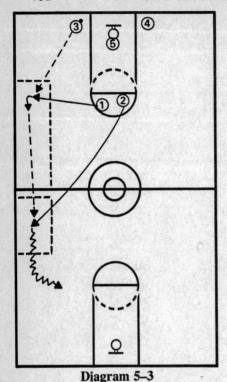

Diagram 5–3

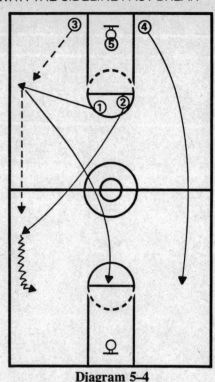

Diagram 5–4

3. If the outlet pass is completed in the area of the foul circle extended, the next offensive player on the top of the floor (usually a guard) breaks to the ball side wing lane, crossing the mid court line, and then looks back to receive a pass from the outlet man (Diagram 5–3). After receiving the pass, this player will also pivot and read, and then begin to dribble the ball up the sideline. If the outlet man does not make this pass, but begins dribbling instead, the man ahead will move to the foul circle and hold this position.

4. When the outlet man passes the ball ahead up the sideline, he then is responsible for filling the middle lane, and whichever player from the weakside of the floor gets there first will fill the other wing lane (Diagram 5–4).

5. If the outlet pass is completed beyond the area of the foul circle extended, the outlet man pivots, reads, and then dribbles the ball up the sideline, and there is to be no crossing of lanes by any other offensive players, with the other outlet man staying in the middle lane (Diagram 5–5).

6. When filling the fast break lanes, the player in the middle

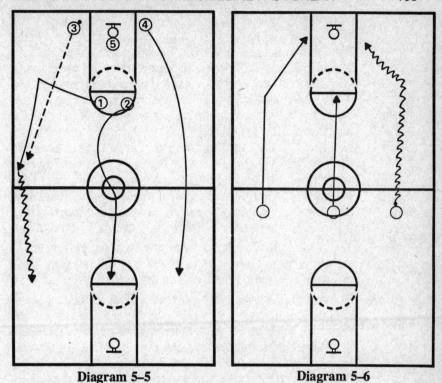

Diagram 5–5   Diagram 5–6

lane will stop at the foul line and wait to see what develops. If he receives a pass from the wing he will take the jump shot if open or hit one of the offensive players in the wing lanes if either is open. The players in the wing lanes break straight down the floor, six to eight feet from the sideline until they reach the area of the foul line extended, then they both make a 45 degree cut to the basket. The reason for this angle cut is so that the backboard can be used on the lay up (Diagram 5–6). Many fast break coaches advocate the wing men moving almost to the baseline and then rounding their cut off and move parallel to the baseline toward the basket. Our only reason for not cutting this way is that we demand the use of the backboard on the lay up, and the rounded cut make this difficult. The player in the wing lane with the basketball will begin to read the defense as he makes his 45 degree angle cut toward the basket, and he must decide, depending on the defense, whether to keep driving toward the basket, stop and take the jump shot, or pass the ball to another lane. Basically, if no defender challenges him, we want the ball handler to keep driving to the basket until he is challenged, by which time he may be in a good enough position to score or to dump the ball off to an open man. If the ball handler is challenged right away we want him to get rid of the ball quickly, because if one defender has come out to stop the ball, we probably have the defense outnumbered somewhere, and we want him to recognize this fact and get rid of the ball so we can take advantage of it. If the defense has overshifted toward the basketball, making a pass difficult, but has not moved out to challenge the ball handler, then the jump shot is in order. The player in the wing lane without the ball will also make a 45 degree angle cut to the basket. If he does not receive a pass he will set up in the low post area on his side of the floor. He must not move across the lane, but hold his position on his own side of the floor.

7. When filling the fast break lanes, the breaking players are to remain eight to ten feet apart all the way up the court, until the wing men begin their cuts to the basket.

8. The fourth offensive player down the floor in the fast break situation is the trailer. If he reaches the scoring area before the break has been completed, he is always to cut to the basket between the middle lane and the wing lane on the ball side and set up in the low post (Diagram 5–7). This is the reason why the player in the wing lane, away from the basketball, is told not to cross over to the ball side. This post area on the ball side is to be left open for the trailer.

9. The last offensive player down the floor in the fast break situation is to stop after crossing the mid court line and take the responsibility for floor balance (Diagram 5–8). If the fast break is not completed, he will then move to his usual front court position,

10. All players in the fast break situation must avoid letting any defensive player force a charging foul on the fast break as this will negate the advantage which the offense is trying to create.

11. Ball handlers in a fast breaking situation are not to leave their feet, unless they are going up on a scoring move. Players who leave their feet out on the floor when they are not in a scoring situation very quickly become victims of the law of gravity. This factor forces them to have to get rid of the basketball before they land in order to avoid a violation. Usually, whatever they do ends up hurting the fast break,

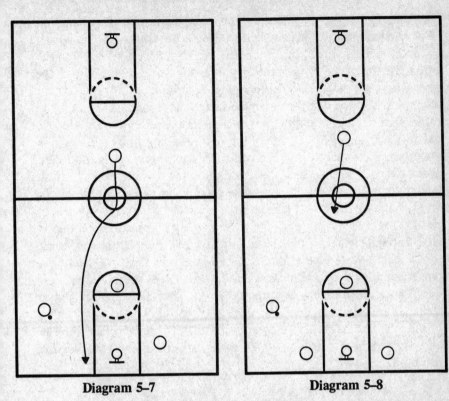

Diagram 5–7   **Diagram 5–8**

either with a bad pass, a forced shot, a charging foul, or a violation. So the fast breaking players are coached to stay on the floor so that they will be able to keep control of the fast break situation.

12. The fast breaking players should complete the break when they outnumber the defense or when they are even with the defense but can get the high percentage shot. This is what the ball handler in the wing lane must be aware of when he makes his 45 degree angle move toward the basket, and as previously mentioned this maneuver puts the ball handler in a floor position to survey the front court situation and determine whether the fast break can be completed or not. If the two fast break situations do not exist in the ball handler's judgment of the situation, then he is expected to get the front court offense set up.

In addition to these principles which are used in trying to establish the concept of control in the sideline fast break, one other method is used to help develop the concept of how fast the fast break is supposed to be carried out. For this concept we divide the court into two zones. From the defensive end of the floor to the top of the foul circle in the offensive end of the floor is referred to as the Speed Zone. This is the zone where we want the offensive players sprinting at full speed in an attempt to beat the defense down the floor. The floor area from the top of the foul circle on into the basket at the offensive end of the floor is called the Control Zone. When the fast breaking players enter this zone, we want them to slow down a little and move at a controlled speed to increase their chances of handling the basketball properly so that any passes and scoring moves will be made by players who have body control, which will increase the chances of carrying out a successful maneuver (Diagram 5–9). Setting up a control zone also is aimed at indoctrinating the players with the concept that the fast break is a quicker hitting type of offense, but it will only be successful if the players control that quickness when they reach the scoring area.

These are the various principles which we have established to create a fast break based on discipline and control. The actual teaching of the sideline fast break is done by means of a series of drills. The purpose of all these drills is to reinforce the principles of the sideline fast break.

SHOOTING DRILLS FOR BUILDING THE BREAK

Drill #1 lay ups

The perfect fast break is the one which results in the uncontested lay up shot. So our first shooting drill for building the fast break is a lay up drill (Diagram 5–10). In this lay up drill, two lines are set up on either side of the floor, starting at the insert line which separates the midcourt from the front court. Both lines have a basketball. I personally believe that it is a complete waste of time to have one line rebound the basketball while the other line shoots, so in this drill both lines are shooting lines, and the shooter is responsible for getting his own rebound and passing the basketball back to the line he came from, and then he switches lines. Of course, if both lines are shooting, a timing pattern must be established to prevent collisions. The first player in the right line begins the drill with a drive to the basket. As soon as this player releases the shot, the player in the left line starts his drive to the basket. This will establish the proper timing so that the drill can be car-

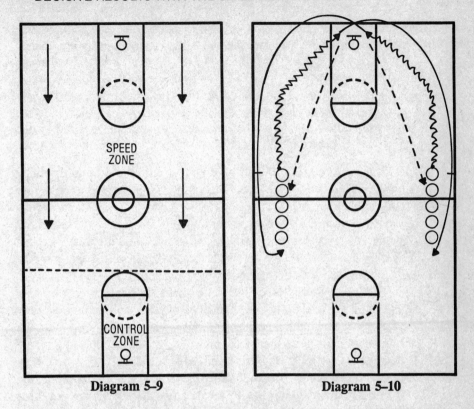

Diagram 5-9   Diagram 5-10

ried out safely. Running the lay up drill in this fashion enables players to shoot twice as many shots as one line shooting would allow, plus it involves the players alternating the lay up shot from right to left throughout the drill.

There are three main points of emphasis for the players to adhere to while executing the lay up drill.

1. The basketball is to be dribbled in a straight line toward the baseline until the player reaches the area of the foul line extended. When the foul line extended is reached, the dribbler is to make a 45 degree angle cut toward the basket and drive in for the lay up shot.

2. In the actual shooting of the lay up, the player is coached to be a high jumper rather than a long jumper, that is we want the lay up shooter going straight up rather than out as he leaves the floor. To develop this technique, the lay up shooter is instructed to lift the knee of his off leg (i.e., the leg on the same side of the shooting hand) up toward the ceiling. This ma-

neuver will ensure that the shooter's body will go straight up in the air, which makes the shot much easier to execute, rather than having the body drift in the air which makes for a more difficult shot.

3. The backboard is to be used for all lay up shots. The player is permitted to release the shot either overhand or underhand, but regardless of the type of release, the player is required to use the backboard.

This lay up drill will also be executed with the players dribbling in, as usual, to the basket, but then coming to a complete stop before shooting, and then using a two foot take off and shooting what is referred to as a power lay up. The power lay up is to be used in those situations in which the player does not have himself under control as he is preparing to shoot the lay up. In this case, the stop and the two foot take off will produce the necessary body control for a balanced shot.

There is also one other principle about shooting the lay up shot which is taught to the players. Our players are not permitted to shoot lay ups going down the middle lane. This is the most difficult of all the lay up shots, and is very easy to miss. Therefore, we do not practice lay ups down the middle. Our players are instructed that anytime they approach the basket down the middle, they are to veer off to either side of the basket and complete the lay up shot by using the backboard. This point may seem to be a minor one, but besides doing away with a very difficult type of shot, it also gives our players just one basic rule to follow on all lay ups, which will eliminate indecision.

Drill #2 loose ball lay ups

In this drill, two lines are again set up, but this time they are formed at opposite ends of the court. One line forms at the insert mark separating mid court from front court, facing the basket farthest away from the line. The other line forms at the insert mark on the other side of the floor, and at the other end of the court (Diagram 5–11).

A basketball is rolled toward the first player in each line. The players pick the ball up on the move and drive to the basket for a lay up. Each player rebounds his own shot, rolls the ball back to the next player in line, and then switches sides. The next player picks the ball up on the move and drives in for the shot, and the drill continues in this manner. The same points of emphasis are followed as in the basic lay up drill, but in this drill, the player must pick the ball up while he is

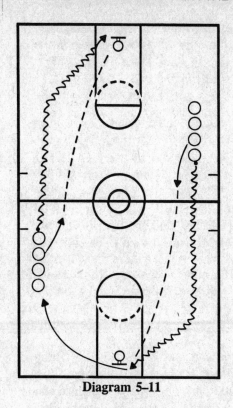

Diagram 5–11

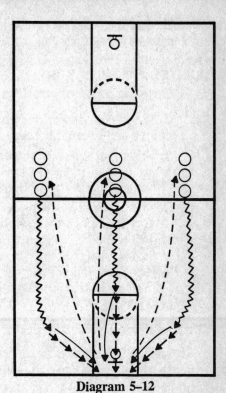

Diagram 5–12

moving, accelerate to full speed while dribbling toward the basket, then slow down when he reaches the control zone around the area of the foul circle extended, make the 45 degree angle cut and drive with control for the lay up shot.

Drill #3 three lane jump shots

The shot most often available in the fast break situation is the 10-15 foot jump shot. So, if a team plans to use the fast break, its players must perfect the techniques of the jump shot from each of the three fast break lanes. That is the purpose of the Three Lane Jump Shot Drill.

The three fast break lanes are formed at half court, and the first player in each line has a basketball. Each player dribbles into the scoring area, takes the jump shot, rebounds, and passes the ball back to his line (Diagram 5-12). In this drill, the players in the wing lanes dribble in a straight line toward the baseline until reaching the foul line extended, they then make a 45 degree cut toward the basket, and after one or two dribbles, stop and take the jump shot. The player in the middle lane dribbles straight to the foul line and takes the jump shot. The players rotate from left to center to right to left.

The main points of emphasis in this drill are:

1. The player is to come under control as he reaches the scoring area and square his body to the basket.
2. The player is to concentrate on proper shooting technique, ball position, grip, hand-arm alignment, sighting, release, and follow through as he takes the jump shot.
3. Special emphasis is placed on the player making sure that he goes straight up in the air on the shot, and that there is no body drift while he is in the air. The shooter is also to be sure that the toes point to the floor and that the feet are not kicked in the air behind the shooter. This area of special emphasis is demanded so that the players will develop a balanced shooting style.

Drill #4 three on none fast break drill

This drill is set up in the same manner as the Three Lane Jump Shot Drill, with the exception that only one basketball is used. This drill is run in two stages. The ball starts in one of the wing lanes and the three fast breaking players move to the scoring area. In the first stage of the drill, the basketball will be passed from the wing lane to the player in the middle lane and he will take the jump shot from the foul line, while both wing men make their proper cut to the basket (Diagram 5–13). The second stage of the drill has the basketball being passed from wing lane to middle lane as above, but the middle man then passes the ball to the other wing lane for that player to shoot a lay up shot (Diagram 5–14).

The points of emphasis in this drill are the same as previously described for the lay up and jump shots. The additional fundamental worked on in this drill is that the fast breaking players will now be receiving a pass while moving in their lanes, and so they must have their hands ready to receive a pass.

BALL HANDLING DRILLS FOR BUILDING THE BREAK

Four ball handling drills are used in the development of the sideline fast break. Although some of the principles of the fast break

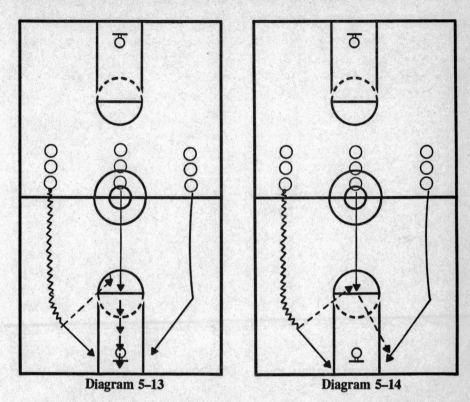

Diagram 5–13   Diagram 5–14

will apply at certain stages of these drills, the primary purpose of each drill is the teaching of the players to be able to pass, hand off, maneuver, and in general, handle the basketball in concert with other players while moving at top speed.

Drill #1 two lane passing

In this drill, the team is divided into two lines which form at the foul line extended in both wing lanes. The drill is first run with a "trainer" basketball, one that is heavier than the regular basketball. The first player in each line will sprint to the other foul line extended, while passing the trainer back and forth (Diagram 5–15). When the two players reach the other foul line extended, they stop, change direction and return to where they started from the same manner, and then the next two players execute the drill.

The points of emphasis:

1. Look the basketball into your hands.
2. Catch the basketball with two hands.

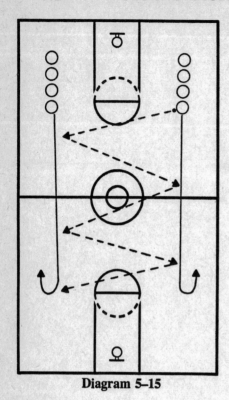

Diagram 5–15

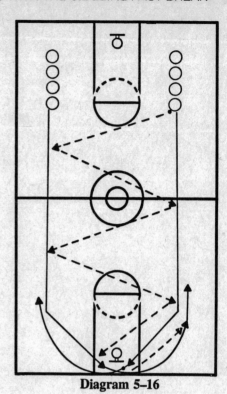

Diagram 5–16

3. Pass the basketball with two hands and from the same plane on which you catch it.

4. Lead your teammate with the pass so that he does not have to break stride when receiving the basketball.

Since there is no shooting sequence in this phase of the drill, we do not continue it past the foul line extended (we do not believe in letting our players shoot with the trainer).

This same drill is then used with a regular basketball. However, when the two players reach the area of the foul line extended, they will make their 45 degree cuts and continue on to the basket, with one of the players shooting the lay up (Diagram 5–16). After the shooter releases his shot, he changes lanes and breaks to the foul line extended, where he waits for an outlet pass. The non-shooter will rebound the shot and outlet the basketball to his teammate, then he changes lanes, and the two players repeat the drill to the other basket. When the sec-

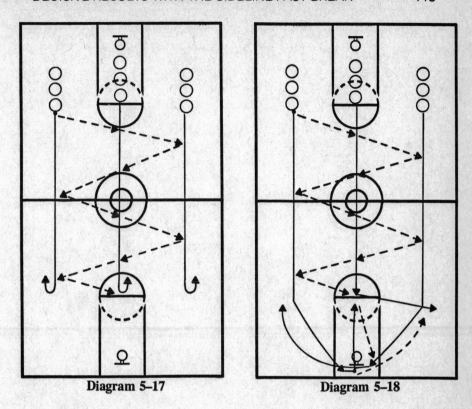

Diagram 5–17   Diagram 5–18

ond lay up shot has been taken, the non-shooter will rebound, as before, but this time he will throw the outlet pass to one of the next players waiting at the foul line extended, and the drill continues with two new players.

Drill #2 three lane passing

This drill is set up the same way as the two lane passing drill, with the addition of a player in the middle lane. In the first phase of the drill a trainer basketball is used. The drill starts at the foul line, with a trainer in one of the wing lanes. The three players sprint to the opposite foul line, passing the trainer back and forth from lane to lane (Diagram 5–17). When they reach the opposite foul line, the three players turn around and repeat the procedure back to the starting point, where three new players will then take over.

The second phase of the drill is to use a regular basketball, and continue on to the basket for a shot. The players will be told whether

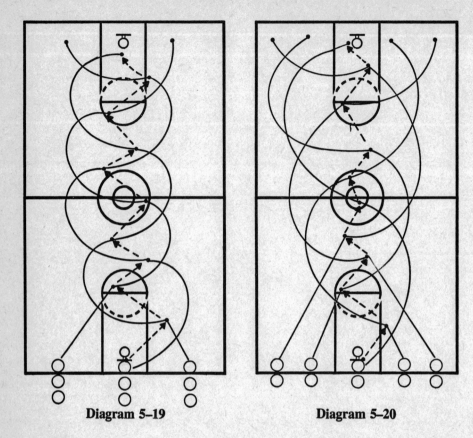

Diagram 5–19   Diagram 5–20

the final pass is to be made to the middle man for the jump shot, or to one of the wing men for the lay up. When the shot is taken, the middle man will move to the outlet area on the side of the rebounder. The rebounder will throw the outlet pass and then fill the wing lane opposite his pass. The non-rebounder will fill the middle lane (Diagram 5–18). The drill is then repeated to the other basket, and after the shot, the outlet pass will be thrown to one of the next players in the outlet area, and the drill is continued by three new players.

The same points of emphasis apply to this drill as in the two lane passing drill. In addition, there is emphasis on the three players moving at full speed until the control area is reached and insistence on the middle man stopping at the foul line and the proper 45 degree cuts by the wing men.

Drill #3 three man weave

This drill is probably one of the oldest of all basketball drills, but for developing good ball handling while players are moving at full speed, it is still one of the best.

The three fast break lanes are filled and the basketball starts in the middle lane. As with the other ball handling drills, the trainer basketball is used first, then the regular basketball is used.

The drill starts with the middle man passing to one of the wings, following his pass and breaking behind the man he passed to. The wing man then passes to the other wing man and follows the same procedure of following the pass and cutting behind the player passed to. This same process of passing, following the pass, and cutting behind the player passed to continues the length of the court (Diagram 5–19). When the opposite baseline is reached, the drill is repeated to the starting point, and three new players take over.

The points of emphasis:

1. Sprint at full speed.
2. Look the ball into your hands.
3. Get rid of the ball quickly with a flip toss to the next receiver, leading him so that he will not have to break stride.

When the regular basketball is used, a lay up shot will be taken.

Drill #4 five man weave

Two more players are now added and a five man weave drill is run. Again the ball starts in the middle. The rule for executing this drill is that the player with the ball flips it to one of the players closest to him, follows his pass, but this time he will cut behind two players (Diagram 5–20). This procedure is followed to the other end of the court and back. The trainer basketball is used first, then the regular basketball, with a shot being taken at each basket.

HALF COURT DRILLS FOR BUILDING THE BREAK

The half court drills are designed to set up the situations which are characteristic of the fast break. They are worked on in a controlled half court situation so that proper player reaction and skill can be developed.

Drill #1 rebound and outlet drill

This drill is designed to develop the basic skills required to initiate

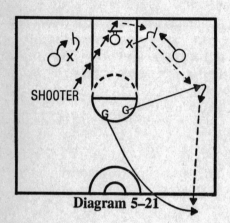

Diagram 5-21

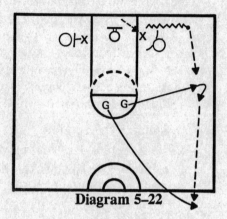

Diagram 5-22

the fast break, getting control of the rebound, and then making a successful outlet pass.

The drill is set up with two offensive rebounders, two defensive rebounders, two outlet men, and a shooter (Diagram 5-21). A rebound ring is placed on the basket.

Two players set up in the area of the foul circle to serve as the outlet men. When the shot is taken, the guards will wait until they see to what side the ball will be rebounded, then the guard on that side breaks to the outlet area, and the other guard will break across mid court and look for the upcourt pass. When the outlet man receives the pass, he is to pivot and look up court as his first move, and then throw a pass to the guard ahead of him.

The ball will be shot from one of the wing areas, so that there will always be a strongside rebounding area and a weakside rebounding area. The strongside rebounder sets up in a denying position on his man. When the shot is taken, the strongside rebounder will read which direction his man is taking to the boards, and then pivot on the foot nearest that direction, make contact with the offensive rebounder, and keep him off the boards. The weakside rebounder will be in a sagging position in the lane when the shot is taken. On the shot, the weakside rebounder is to step out toward his man, so that he will not be pinned too far inside when the ball rebounds. As the weakside rebounder steps out, he is to read the direction of the offensive rebounder, pivot on the foot nearest that direction, make contact, and keep his man off the boards. The defensive rebounders are to use both hands when gaining possession of the basketball.

When the rebound has been secured by the defensive rebounder, he is to turn toward the sideline and look for the outlet man. The rebounder's primary job now is to complete the outlet pass. If he meets no defensive pressure, he will release the basketball immediately to the outlet man who will have established a passing lane. If one of the offensive rebounders tries to deny the outlet pass, the rebounder is to dribble toward the sideline, relieve this pressure, and get the ball to the outlet man, who once again must work to create a passing lane (Diagram 5–22).

The emphasis in this drill is on the rebounder establishing and maintaining a good block out position, and after gaining control of the rebound, making sure that the basketball reaches the outlet area safely. For the two outlet men, the emphasis is on not leaving the foul circle until the basketball has been rebounded by one of their teammates. Then they are to move to the proper areas in the outlet area and into the front court. The outlet man is to establish a passing lane, and after re-

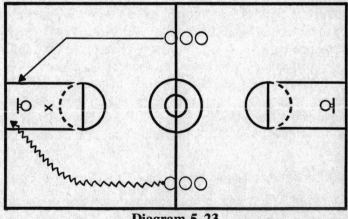

Diagram 5–23

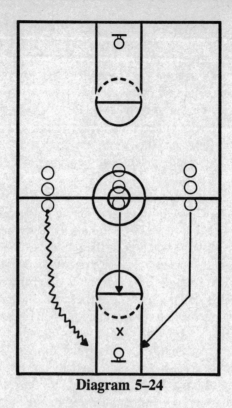

Diagram 5–24

ceiving the pass, pivot, find the next upcourt receiver, and complete the pass to him.

The Rebound and Outlet Drill is run with five shots being taken from one side of the floor, then the shooter moves to the other wing area and five shots are taken from the other side of the floor. The other players in the drill maintain their same court position and this way they have the opportunity to work on the strongside of the floor for half of the drill, and then on the weakside for the rest of the drill. After completion of the ten shots, the two offensive rebounders become the defensive rebounders, and two new outlet men take over. The two defensive rebounders leave the drill. All of the players, whether they be guards or inside players, take a turn at both the rebounding and outlet spots.

Drill #2 two on one half court fast break

This drill is designed to teach the proper offensive reactions for the 2 on 1 fast break situation, and teach these reactions in a controlled half court drill, so that the total concentration is on the 2 on 1 phase of the break and nothing else.

Two lines are formed at mid court in the two wing lanes. The two wing lanes are used because in a 2 on 1 situation we want the two breaking players in the wing lanes so that the one defender has to cover as much court space as possible. One defender sets up in the lane area. The ball is dribbled in from the mid court area and the 2 on 1 fast break is executed (Diagram 5–23).

These are the principles to be followed when carrying out the 2 on 1 fast break:

1. The dribbler must force the defender to make a choice. If the defender attacks the dribbler, the dribbler is to pass off to his teammate. If the defender takes the other cutter or tries to stay in the middle and play both men, then the dribbler is to take the ball all the way to the basket.

2. The basic principle of the 2 on 1 fast break situation is that the two offensive players are always to get the lay up shot. No one is ever to stop and take the jump shot, only lay ups are permitted in the 2 on 1 situation.

3. The dribbler is not to leave his feet unless he is going up for the lay up shot. The player who leaves the floor gives up the offensive advantage of the 2 on 1 situation, so the offensive players are instructed to stay on the floor so that they can take advantage of the fact that the defense is outnumbered.

4. Neither breaking player must let the defender force them into a charging foul, as this will cost them an almost certain basket.

5. The players must make an effort to complete the 2 on 1 fast break with one pass. In some situations two passes can be used, but more than two passes will permit defensive help to arrive and the outnumbering situation will be gone. This one pass guideline, of course, depends on the play of the defender. If he makes no effort to stop the dribbler, then the dribbler is not expected to pass off, but to take the ball to the basket himself.

The rotation for this drill has the player in the right wing lane becoming the defender after his turn on offense, the left wing player moves to the right wing, and the defender moves to the left wing.

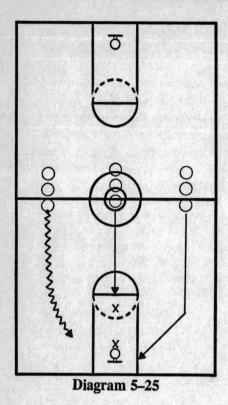

Diagram 5–25

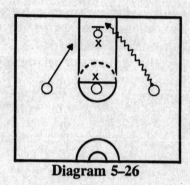

Diagram 5–26

Drill #3 three on one half court fast break

In this drill all three of the fast break lanes are filled. Again this drill is worked on the half court area so that there is concentration on just the scoring phase. One defender is positioned in the lane area. The basketball, as usual, is in one of the wing lanes. The ball is advanced in the wing lane into the scoring area. The player in the middle lane stops at the foul line, while the players in the wing lanes make their 45 degree cuts to the basket (Diagram 5–24).

The same points of emphasis are followed in the 3 on 1 situation as in the 2 on 1. The basic objective is to get the lay up shot. No jump shots are to be taken, and no more than two passes should be thrown, if any passes are necessary. The rotation for the drill is from left wing to middle to right wing to defense to left wing.

Drill#4 three on two half court fast break

The 3 on 2 fast break is probably the most common of all the fast

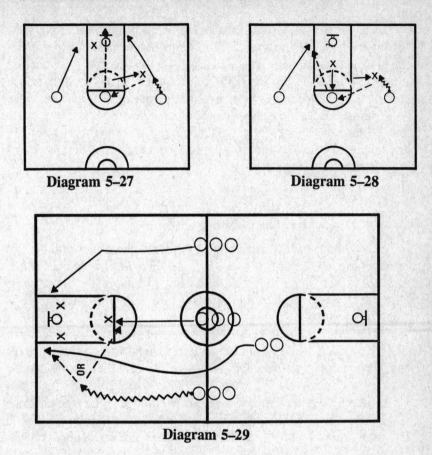

Diagram 5–27   Diagram 5–28

Diagram 5–29

break situations. So the next step in building the break on a half court basis is to develop proper offensive reactions for the 3 on 2 situation. The drill is set up in the same way as the 3 on 1 drill, with the addition of a second defender. The ball is advanced along the sideline (Diagram 5–25), and the dribbler must read what the defense is trying to do. As with the other fast break situations, the dribbler is to attack the defense and force them to do something. If the defense does not challenge him he is to drive to the basket, which sets up the situation in which he has bypassed the top defender and created a 2 on 1 situation (Diagram 5–26). If the defender on top moves out to challenge the dribbler, the middle lane will be left open for the jump shot from the foul line (Diagram 5–27). And if the bottom defender tries to move up and deny this shot, the weakside cutter will be open (Diagram 5–28).

It is in the 3 on 2 situation that the real advantage of moving the ball along the sideline shows up. The dribbler is able to get much closer to the basket before the defense stops him, and this fact enables the other offensive players to move closer to the basket as well, which puts them in better scoring position and increases the chances of the break being successful. The rotation for this drill is for the two wing men to move to defense, the middle man moves to the right lane, one defender will move to the middle lane, and the other defender will move to the left wing.

Drill #5 four on three half court fast break

The 4 on 3 drill is used next to introduce the trailer into the fast break situation. The drill is set up with the three fast break lanes filled, three defenders in the lane area, and a line of trailers positioned some 8-10 feet behind the middle lane. All four offensive players break when the dribbler begins his advance along the sideline. The trailer's rule is that he is to break to the low post position on the ball side of the floor (Diagram 5–29). As previously mentioned, the dribbler is responsible for reading the defense and making sure that the offense gets the best shot possible. The trailer is also instructed that if a pass has been made by the time he reaches the foul circle area, he is to continue down the lane on the side where the ball entered the scoring area. With this as his rule, the trailer does not have to be concerned about changing lanes. The rotation for this drill has the trailer moving to the middle lane, the defenders to the two wing lanes and the trailer line, and the three lane men to defense.

These are the five half court drills which are used to develop the various phases of the fast break. Many coaches do not believe that the fast break should be taught on a half court basis, since it is a full court occurrence. However, I believe that if you want a fast break with control, the half court drills will teach the basic fast break fundamentals and principles in such a way that when the fast break becomes a full court occurrence, the reactions developed by these half court drills will give the fast break that element of control. This is due to the fact that the fundamentals, principles, and guidelines for the fast break will have been developed in a controlled learning situation. This type of controlled learning setup enables the players to learn when the fast break situation exists and should be completed and when it does not

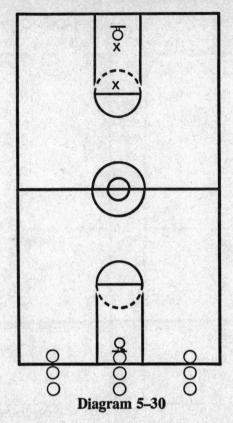

Diagram 5–30

exist and should not be concluded. It is this type of player recognition which leads to the development of a mental control in the players which prevents the fast break from getting out of hand. In our experience, these half court drills have been extremely worthwhile in developing a controlled fast break because they create both a mental and physical learning experience, and for this reason they serve as one of the basic building blocks in the overall development of the controlled, sideline fast break.

FULL COURT DRILLS FOR BUILDING THE BREAK

Two full court drills are used to combine the various fundamentals of the fast break and put them into operation on a full court basis. These drills are still a controlled approach to the fast break since they involve only five or six players at a time, but now these players must react to a full court fast break situation with outlet passes, advancement of the ball along the sideline into the scoring area, and then recognition

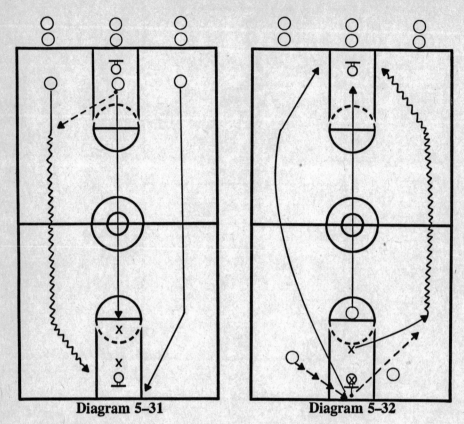

Diagram 5–31   Diagram 5–32

of the defensive play followed by the proper offensive choice to complete the break. Both of these drills are hustling, full speed types of drills. No boundaries are used, so the ball is always in play, which encourages hustle everywhere to get to the basketball. The drills do not stop after a successful shot, for the ball is rebounded as it comes through the net by one of the defenders and he will outlet the ball, and the drill continues with no break in the action.

Drill #1 three on two, two on one continuous fast break

    For this drill the players line up in the three fast break lanes at one end of the floor. Two players are sent to the other end of the floor to play defense, (Diagram 5–30). This drill starts with the player in the middle lane throwing an outlet pass to one of the players in the wing area. The basketball is then advanced along the sideline with the three breaking players moving at full speed until they reach the control zone.

They then attack the two defenders according to the principles of the 3 on 2 situation (Diagram 5–31).

When this offensive sequence is completed, either with a basket, or with the defense gaining possession of the basketball, the two defenders now become the offensive players, fill the two wing lanes and begin a fast break toward the other basket. The player in the first fast break sequence, who was in the middle lane and stopped at the foul line, now becomes the defender and must retreat to the other basket and play defense against the two fast breaking players (Diagram 5–32). The two players who were in the wing lanes in the 3 on 2 sequence remain at the basket which they broke to, and become the defenders against the next group of three players.

As the 2 on 1 sequence reaches the scoring area, the next players in the wing lane lines begin moving out on the floor toward the outlet areas. The middle man remains out of bounds, under the basket. If the shot is made in the 2 on 1 break, the middle man will grab the basketball as it comes through the net and throw an outlet pass which will start the next 3 on 2 break. If the lone defender gains possession of the basketball, by means of a rebound or interception, he will outlet the basketball, and the middle man will fill the middle lane and start the 3 on 2 sequence of this drill (Diagram 5–33).

The 3 on 2, 2 on 1 sequence goes on continuously, and because of this it is not only a good conditioner, but it creates fast break situations from both rebounds and turnovers, and since no boundaries are used the basketball is always in play, and this ensures that this drill will be a continuous drill.

Drill #2 the fast break drill

The second full court drill used for developing the fast break is simply called the fast break drill. I believe that this is the finest fast break drill available, and if I were limited to only one fast break drill, this is the one I would choose. This drill is the favorite drill of both players and coaches, and so when this drill is run a lot of effort, energy, and enthusiasm are put into it. The fast break drill is run in two stages. For the first stage of the drill, which is a continuous 3 on 2 fast break, at least 11 players are required. For the second stage, in which a trailer is added to produce a 4 on 3 fast break, at least 14 players are needed.

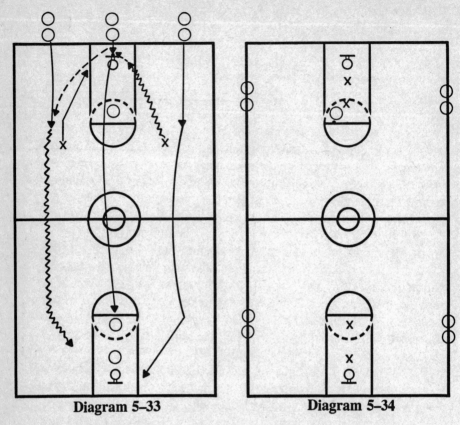

Diagram 5-33　　　　　　**Diagram 5-34**

　　　The first stage of the drill, the 3 on 2 sequence is practiced more often than the second stage. This drill is set up as shown in Diagram 5-34. Two defenders are positioned at each basket. The remaining players split up and station themselves out of bounds, along the sidelines, in the vicinity of the foul lines extended. One player, with a basketball, will position himself just below the foul circle. One player from each of the sidelines at this end of the court will step in bounds. The middle man will outlet the ball to one of them and this begins the 3 on 2 fast break sequence (Diagram 5-35). When the three breaking players reach the scoring area, one player from each sideline at that end of the floor moves in bounds and positions himself in an outlet area. As soon as the fast break sequence is completed with either a successful shot, a defensive rebound, or a turnover, the defender who gains possession of the basketball will pass to one of the outlet areas. The player who receives the outlet pass will pivot upcourt and look before advancing. The outlet man who did not receive the pass, sprints to the middle

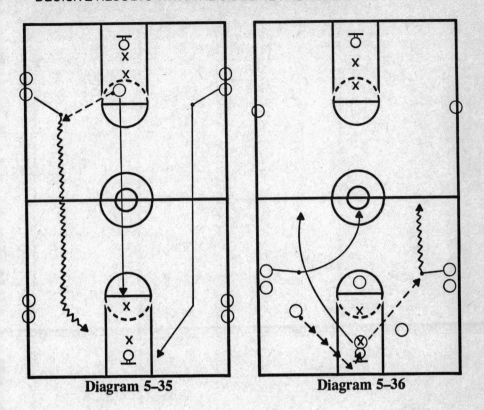

Diagram 5–35   **Diagram 5–36**

lane. The defender who threw the outlet pass becomes the third man in the fast break and fills the wing lane opposite his outlet pass (Diagram 5–36).

If the player who fills the middle lane can get ahead of the basketball, he will leave the middle lane and sprint into the ball side wing lane. When this situation occurs, the outlet man passes the ball ahead and he then fills the middle lane (Diagram 5–37). If the player in the middle lane cannot get ahead of the ball, all the players stay in their lanes and the outlet man dribbles the ball into the scoring area. Now another 3 on 2 situation has been developed, and the same procedure is followed as previously described. The drill is a continuous one in which the players develop the skills of making the outlet pass, filling the fast break lanes, advancing the basketball through the speed and control zones, and concluding with the reading of the defensive play so that the proper offensive reaction can be made to produce the best chance of scoring. As each fast break sequence ends, the two wing

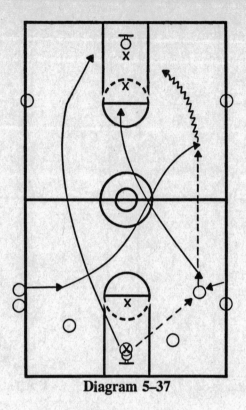

Diagram 5–37

men go to defense while the middle man and the defender who did not throw the outlet pass go to the sideline areas.

The second stage of the drill is a 4 on 3 situation, which introduces the trailer into the fast break sequence. The drill is set up as previously described, with the addition of a third defender at each basket. The defenders decide among themselves which two will take part in the break. The drill starts with a 2 on 3 situation, and when the break is completed, a continuous 4 on 3 sequence begins. One of the two designated defenders will fill a wing lane when the fast break starts the other way, and the other defender will become the trailer, breaking to the low post on the ball side (Diagram 5–38). The players who filled the three fast break lanes become the defenders when their break ends, while the trailer and the remaining defender move to the sideline area.

As with the 3 on 2, 2 on 1 fast break drill, there are no boundaries, the basketball is always in play, so it is a good idea to have all the bleachers pushed in, the doors locked, and the windows closed. Then

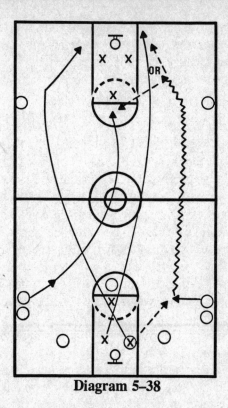

Diagram 5-38

get out of the players way and let them go, and you will be amazed at the effort which they will put forth in these drills.

TEAM FAST BREAK

With the various build up drills completed, we are now ready to approach the fast break from a team standpoint. Two types of drills are used in which a complete offense and a complete defense are used. So far, in all the previous fast break drills, the offense has always had the numerical advantage, which usually leads to the successful completion of the break. Now with a total team set up, the offense no longer has this advantage at the start of the drill. The offense has to work to establish a fast break opportunity, and once it has been established, the offense now is faced with making the judgment of whether the fast break should be completed or whether the front court offense should be set up. The fast breaking players now face the situation in which they must read whether the offense outnumbers the defense or whether they are equal with the defense, but can get the good shot. In both of these cases the break is to be carried through to its completion. But the breaking players also must identify the situation when these cases do not exist, and must then move into the designated front court offense as quickly as possible.

Drill #1 five on five

The five on five fast break drill is basically a controlled scrimmage type of drill. One team is placed on offense, the other is designated as the defensive. The offense runs either one of our own front court offenses, or that of an opponent, while the defensive team uses one of our front court defenses. If the offense scores, the basketball goes back out to mid court and is given to the offense again. When the defense gains possession of the basketball by means of a rebound, interception, or steal, they will immediately try to establish a fast break situation, and the offensive team will attempt to get back on defense and stop the break. The players of the fast breaking team are now faced with making the judgment as to whether the fast break should be completed or whether the front court offense should be set up. When this sequence is completed the drill is stopped, and corrections can be made or advice given on the part of the coaches. Then the two teams switch roles with the fast breaking team going on offense. The other team goes on defense and will try to establish a fast break situation. The final fast break principle which comes into play now is that the last member of the fast breaking team to reach the front court must stop after reaching the mid court area and take the responsibility for floor balance. If no shot is taken off the fast break, then he will move into his normal offensive position.

Drill #2 group fast break

This team fast break drill is also run in a controlled scrimmage set up. The junior varsity team is used in this drill, and they will always be the offensive team, with the responsibility of trying to stop the fast break when they lose possession of the basketball. The varsity squad is then divided into two or three groups, depending on the number of players on the team. The starting unit is placed on defense against the junior varsity then runs a front court offense, maintaining possession of the basketball when they score. When the defense gains possession, they will attempt to fast break, and when reaching the scoring area, make the judgment of whether to complete the break or set up in a front court offense. If they set up in a front court offense, they will run it through to completion. Then the ball is given back to the junior varsity and the varsity squad goes back on defense and the same procedure is followed. When the second fast break sequence has been completed, the first varsity group is replaced by the second group, and then they will go through this up and back sequence, and then they will be replaced. As the drill continues, the personnel of each group can be changed so that different combinations have the opportunity of playing together.

That concludes the description of the various drills which are used to put the sideline type of fast break together. Since the sideline break is one that is based on the element of control, these drills have been devised so that they teach the specific skills required of the fast break on a half court and then full court basis, but always in a controlled situation. We believe that this is the type of environment which is necessary to develop player discipline and control, but at the same time create an offensive attack which is capable of producing that quick and decisive spurt of baskets.

In teaching the fast break, probably more than in any other phase of the game, the coach must have patience, because it is a difficult process for players to learn the proper reaction and judgment. This patience is especially necessary for the coach who is installing the controlled style of fast break, because that coach must put his players through fast break situation after fast break situation so that they learn to make the decision of when to complete the break and when to set up, because that is the key decision on which the fast break with control rests. The players must learn that merely starting the fast break does not automatically mean that it must be carried through to its conclusion. Instead, they must develop a tactical approach to the fast break and learn that the fast break is completed only when it is to their advantage to do so. The coach must convince his players that the fast break is just one of the offensive weapons which they have at their disposal and should be used with that knowledge and not be forced, because they still have an effective front court attack which will produce the high percentage shot eventually.

The fast break is the icing on the cake. It is that extra weapon which creates additional problems for the defense. The coach who has the patience to teach the controlled fast break will be rewarded. All the time spent on the drills to develop the fast break with control will give the coach the ultimate offensive weapon, the offensive weapon which will seek to gain the advantage over the defense, which assures the high percentage shot, but an offensive weapon which is used with discipline and control, and will not be forced when the advantage is not there.

The fast break adds effectiveness to a team's total offensive system, because it gives the defense another offensive attack to confront. The sideline fast break has been a most effective style of break, because it threatens the defense from within a framework of discipline and control. As such, the sideline fast break is another stepping stone to the goal of achieving court control.

6

ATTACKING AND CONTROLLING PRESSURE DEFENSES

STRATEGY FOR ATTACKING PRESSURE

Pressure defense is becoming more and more a basic approach of basketball defenses. It is easy to understand why this is so. Today's basketball players from high school to the pros have become so skilled offensively that they simply cannot be permitted freedom of movement to do what they want to do. An obvious way of attempting to take away this offensive freedom is to use some kind of defensive pressure, either full court, half court, or both to make it as difficult as possible for the offensive player to operate at his accustomed floor position or at his accustomed pace. Spreading out the offense and making it react to various types of pressure maneuvers can be very upsetting and so can take away some of the offensive effectiveness of the modern basketball player, that is, it can take away that effectiveness if the offense does not have a planned method for attacking pressure. If a plan is available, and the offensive players recognize, react, and carry out the plan, then the defensive strategy can be defeated.

Our basic approach in attacking and controlling pressure defense, regardless of where it is applied and regardless of whether it is man, zone, combination, run and jump, etc., is to convince our players that the pressure defense is first of all, a type of psychological warfare. The pressure defense attempts to put so much pressure on the ball handler that he becomes flustered. He begins to worry about ten second or five second counts, he wants to get rid of the basketball as quickly as possible, he panics, throws the ball up for grabs, and the pressure defense has succeeded in its objective. So the first teaching step for our players is to impress upon them that to attack and control the various kinds of pressure defense they must maintain their poise at all times. This poise will enable them to read the defense and then pick it apart.

To create this necessary poise, we establish a definite set of rules or principles to be followed when attacking pressure. Having these guidelines to follow enables the individual player to develop a sense of security when confronted by pressure defenses, because he knows what is expected of him and what to expect from his teammates. It is the creation of this sense of security in the individual which leads to the development of poise under pressure.

PRINCIPLES FOR ATTACKING PRESSURE

1. The most important principle used in attacking pressure is that the offensive team should not hurry things at the beginning. Whether the defense is using full or half court pressure, our players are taught not to try and hurry the basketball into play against the pressure defense. Instead, they are to let the defense set up, and then after it has been set the offense begins its attack.

2. Against full court pressure, the designated player is to always take the ball out of bounds, and the immediate in bounds receivers must align as high as the foul line. This floor position will give the receivers enough room to work to get open, and in moving to get open they are instructed to make angle cuts.

3. When attacking pressure defenses, pass receivers are always to move toward the ball to prevent defenders from being able to move in for the interception.

4. Avoid the use of bounce or lob passes when advancing the basketball. They are too slow and invite the interception.

5. Cross court passes should be no longer than 8-10 feet. Any greater distance may result in an interception. One exception

to this principle is that the diagonal pass from on top of the floor to the opposite low post is permitted when a scoring opportunity presents itself against half court pressure. Straight ahead passes (i.e. up the court) can be longer than 8-10 feet.

6. Don't dribble merely for the sake of dribbling. Dribble to attack the defense or to advance the basketball. Read the defense as you dribble and get the basketball to the open man at the first opportunity. More dribbling can be used against man to man pressure, less dribbling should be used against zone pressure.

7. Move toward the trap, and then pass the basketball before it is set.

8. Attack pressure defenses with two objectives in mind:

   a) First, attempt to penetrate the defense. Penetration will result in bypassing one or two or more defenders, which will then give the offense the numerical advantage which then creates the fast break situation.

   b) If penetration is impossible, reverse the basketball and advance it, looking for the first opportunity to penetrate. If penetration remains unattainable, continue the reversing and advancing process.

This principle establishes the strategy of swinging the basketball from side to side as the offense moves up the court, making the defense move with us. If the defense leaves the middle open, we will throw a penetrating pass and attack quickly. If the middle does not open up, the reversing of the basketball will enable us to maneuver into the front court, and then set up a front court offense.

The basic thinking behind these principles is that the offense is taught to think "attack" when confronted by pressure, but the attack is not a free lance racing up the court. The attack is under control because each player knows what to expect of his teammate. The offense is coached not to be in a hurry to initiate offensive action which might lead to a bad pass, a quick interception, a violation or some other type of turnover. Instead, the offense is to align itself in the designated attacking formation, and only after the proper alignment has been established should the offensive attack begin. Then, when the offense has been initiated from the proper alignment, and the opportunity is presented for penetration, followed by the chance to create an advantageous offensive situation, the offense is expected to do just that. However, this is to be done only after setting up, getting the ball safely in bounds, and then reading the defense to see if the opportunity for penetration is there. We want our players to develop court awareness, court sense, and court control. They are taught that after the attacking formation has been established they are to look immediately for the chance to blitz the defense and move the basketball quickly down the floor and create a fast break situation. But at the same time the players must have enough awareness to realize when the quick attack is not there. In this situation they must be taught not to force the attack, but rather begin a series of offensive maneuvers which will control the pressure defense and force them to retreat until they are forced into a front court defensive situation, and they can then be attacked with a front court offense. The control phase of the attack is the swinging or the reversing of the basketball from side to side, moving toward the trap, then getting rid of the basketball before it is set, which forces the defense to retreat and readjust. While this reversing action is taking place, the offense is ever alert to the opportunity to penetrate at any time, thus giving the offense a method of attack which can shift gears or tempo whenever the opportunity is available.

If the offensive team can avoid getting caught in the psychological environment which the pressure defense is trying to produce and can maintain a controlled composure, pressure defense can be handled, and the good percentage shots will result.

This atmosphere can be created by developing relatively simple methods of attack against full and half court pressure defenses, methods of attack which place the players into court positions from which the offense will have the opportunity for penetration with the basketball first, and reversal of the basketball second. When the offensive players come to the realization that these two options will always be available to them, the fear of pressure defense will disappear. In its place will appear a confident feeling that no matter what kind of pressure defense may be used, it can be attacked and controlled. The development of the individual confidence of each player is the first step in breaking down the psychological value of the pressure defense.

OFFENSIVE METHODS FOR CONTROLLING
HALF COURT PRESSURE

We identify the half court press as the type of defense which is set up at the mid court line or close to it, in which the objective of the defense is to establish some kind of trapping situation. Thus, a straight man to man with tough half court pick up is not regarded as a half court press, and we expect our offensive players to be able to maneuver against such a defense into a normal front court offense. It is only those various zones or man to man trapping defenses which we consider as half court presses, and which are to be attacked by our half court pressure offense.

The offensive set against the half court press is our basic 2-1-2 alignment, with the only adjustment being the position of the high post player. The high post, O5, will align at the top of the foul circle (Diagram 6–1) rather than at his usual position at the foul line.

Regardless of the type of half court press which is being used, we want the basketball to be advanced up the side of the court. The guard without the basketball is to remain several steps behind the line of the ball so that he is always a constant outlet man for the dribbler. The reason for advancing the basketball along the side of the court is that we want to force the defense to commit itself to one side of the floor and then attack them before they can totally take away our offensive possibilities. So the dribbler will advance the basketball toward a trapping area, entice the defense to move to trap the ball, and then move the basketball to one of four designated attack areas before the trap can be set. As the dribbler moves toward the front court, both the strongside forward, O4, and the high post, O5, move out higher on the floor, while the weakside forward, O3, holds his spot (Diagram 6–2). As these offensive maneuvers are being carried out, the dribbler, O2, will be reading the defense, and considering four attack areas, in this priority:

1. penetrating pass to high post area.
2. long lob pass to weakside forward.
3. outside penetrating pass to strongside forward.
4. reverse pass to weakside guard.

A pass to any one of these attack areas will initiate a sequence of offensive moves designed to produce a high percentage shot, which is unquestionably the most psychologically damaging event that can befall pressing defenses.

PENETRATING PASS TO THE HIGH POST AREA

The primary offensive attack against the half court press is to get the basketball into the high post area. Such penetration usually results

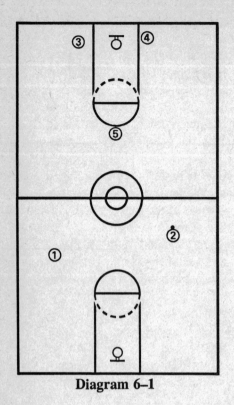

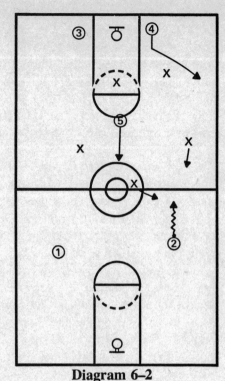

Diagram 6–1   Diagram 6–2

in the offense gaining a numerical advantage near the basket area with a basic fast break situation being produced. The dribbler, O2, will recognize that this opportunity is available when he reads trapping action moving toward the ball, while at the same time a weakside defender moves to deny the pass to O1 (Diagram 6–3). When the penetrating pass is made to O5, that player is to pivot immediately upon reception and face the basket. This turning move is emphasized so that the high post will not get into the habit of pivoting and immediately putting the basketball on the floor, in which case he might miss the open man underneath or draw a charging foul if a defender has moved in behind him after the pass reception. As this penetrating pass is being made, O4 will break back toward the basket, which will hopefully create a 3 on 2 situation. O5 is to pass the ball to either post area if either player is open (Diagram 6–4). If neither player is open, O5 should then be able to dribble the basketball to the foul line for the 15 foot jump shot (Diagram 6–5), but always being ready to move the ball inside if one of the defenders challenges him.

138

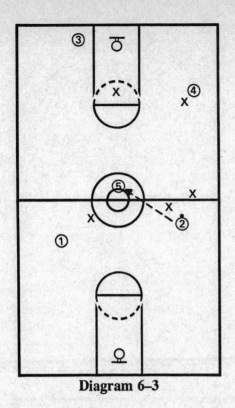

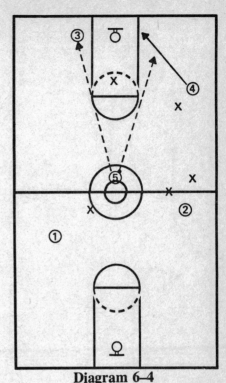

| Diagram 6–3 | Diagram 6–4 |

After the offense has successfully penetrated the defense in this manner several times, the defense will now become concerned with denying the pass to the high post player, and most likely they will try to do this by dropping the defender who has been covering O1 into the high post area. When this defensive adjustment is made, O5 is instructed to read it and clear out toward the ball side of the floor, while O3 breaks to the top of the key (Diagram 6–6). Once again O4 goes to the basket, If a defender does not follow O5, the basketball can be passed to him with little difficulty, since the inside defender on that side of the floor will have to sag with the breaking O4. If the basketball is passed to O5, he pivots toward the basket and reads the defense, hitting the open man or dribbling toward the basket if no passing situation is available to him. One additional maneuver which the offense makes in this situation is that as soon as the ball is passed to O5 along the sidelines, O1 breaks to the weakside low post, which now gives O5 three passing options (Diagram 6–7). The ball passed inside should result in a lay up shot; the ball passed to the middle produces the 3 on 2

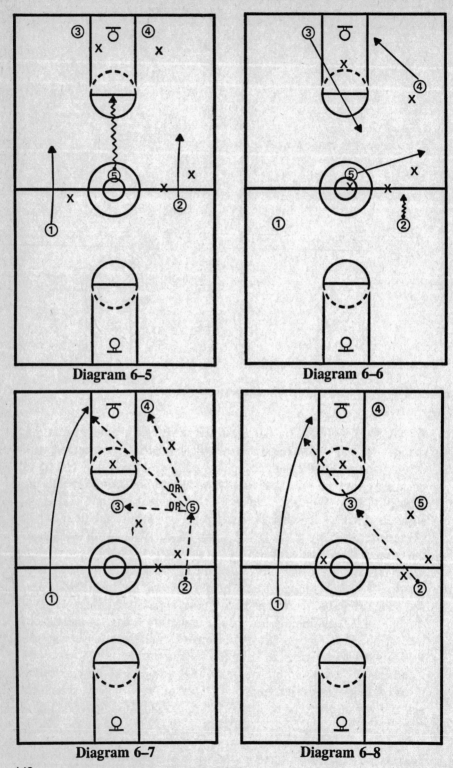

Diagram 6–5

Diagram 6–6

Diagram 6–7

Diagram 6–8

situation as previously described, but this time with different players involved.

On the other hand, if the defender goes with O5 when he clears to the sideline, O2 will now look to make the pass to O3, who is breaking to the top of the key area, and with O1 cutting to the basket as this pass is made, a back door lay up will often be the result (Diagram 6–8). O3, like O5, is taught to pivot and read before dribbling, and in this situation will be looking for O1 cutting to the basket. If the inside defenders drop to defend against this move, O3 is now in position to dribble to the foul line and take advantage of another 3 on 2 situation (Diagram 6–9).

LONG LOB PASS TO WEAKSIDE FORWARD

The attack directed toward the middle of the half court press is the primary means of defeating the pressure situation, but court control is better assured when multiple options are available to combat various methods of defensive play. So the second priority in the attack against the half court press is the achievement of the ultimate in penetration, by bypassing the entire defense with the long lob pass.

As the defense begins to recognize our basic strategy against their half court press, they will gradually begin to position themselves so that they can pressure the pass into the high post, while at the same time denying the basketball to the weakside guard. To do this they must leave the weakside forward open, but since he is the most removed player from the basketball, it seems to be a reasonable gamble.

However, O2 is taught to be aware of this situation when it develops. He is to constantly scan the defense as he moves toward the trapping area, and when he reads this defensive adjustment, he is to fire the long lob pass immediately to O3 for the easy lay up (Diagram 6–10). Since all of our players practice throwing this kind of pass, we are not caught unprepared when this situation arises, and so our guards have no hesitation about putting the ball in the air in an attempt to go over the top of the defense. This pass thrown successfully just once will usually cause the defense to drop back again, which opens the middle once again and lets the offense attack with the basic penetrating sequence. So the threat of the long lob pass has a controlling effect on the defense, for here in a situation where the defense is trying to seize the initiative with their pressure, the knowledge that the offense will throw the long lob pass against them has a controlling effect on their

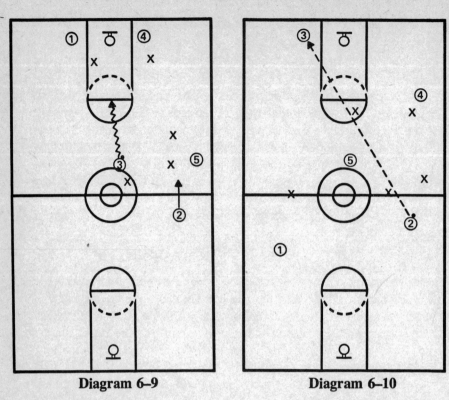

Diagram 6-9   Diagram 6-10

aggressiveness and keeps the inside defenders hanging back, thus opening the other areas of penetration.

OUTSIDE PENETRATING PASS TO THE STRONGSIDE FORWARD

If the defense now decides to defend the middle area, while at the same time denying the long lob pass, the strongside forward will be the open man. O2 must recognize this defensive action and penetrate along the perimeter of the defense with a pass to O4, the offensive players will immediately execute the Regular Zone Offense pattern, with the only difference being that the guards will not change sides of the floor. So when the pass is made to O4, O5 will break down the lane on the ball side and set up in the strongside low post, while O3 flashes high to the foul line. If a pass is made to either of these cutters; O1 will break backdoor to the weakside low post (Diagram 6-11). Usually these maneuvers will produce a good percentage shot. If not, the defense will have been forced into a front court defense situation, and they can then be attacked with one of the front court offenses.

REVERSE PASS TO THE WEAKSIDE GUARD

When none of these first three passing priorities are open to the

142

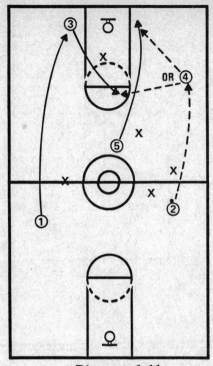

Diagram 6–11

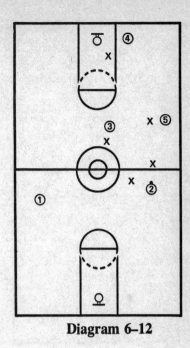

Diagram 6–12

strongside guard, he immediately knows that the basketball is to be reversed to the weakside guard, since the defense will have to leave him open if they are trying to trap the ball while cutting off the other three passing options. As the ball is reversed to O1, the offensive set will have O5 on the opposite sideline and O3 in the middle of the floor (Diagram 6–12), since they will have moved to these positions in the course of the offensive movement as previously described. When O1 receives the pass from O2, he will usually be able to dribble into the front court without facing much defensive pressure. This action will force the defense to drop back into some kind of front court defense. However, the offense does not wait for the defense to readjust. As O1 advances the basketball, O3 will move from the middle of the floor and break to the ball side wing area, while O5 returns from the sideline position to his normal area of operation at the foul line (Diagram 6–13). From this alignment, the offense then moves into the Regular Zone Offense. The basketball is passed to O3, O5 rolls down the lane on the ball side, O4 flashes high, while the guards remain on the same side of the floor, with O2 being ready to cut to the basket area if a penetrating pass is made (Diagram 6–14). If the good percentage shot does not result, the ball will be brought back outside, and since the defense is now

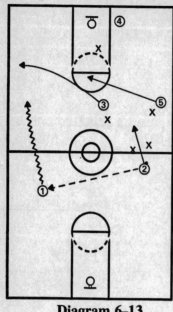

Diagram 6–13

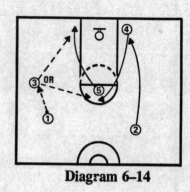

Diagram 6–14

forced to remain in a front court defense, the offense can now renew its attack with one of the front court offenses.

These four passing options, each of which takes advantage of various defensive maneuvers, comprise the offense against the half court press. It is a simple attack, but with the proper read from the strongside guard, an effective attack which enables the offense to control defensive pressure because there is always an option available regardless of the defensive maneuver.

INSTALLING THE HALF COURT PRESS OFFENSE

The offense against the half court press is installed on a team drill basis. First the basic strategy of the offense is explained, then the tactics of the offense are dealt with by aligning players in the offensive set and explaining the passing options and the priorities. The various offensive movements are then walked through from each passing option. Next the offense is executed without a defense, with all the passing possibilities being covered. By now the players will have a basic understanding of the kinds of offensive situations to look for, and so it is time to add five defenders. The defenders are organized into some kind of half court press, and the offense attacks them.

We have found that the team approach in attacking the half court press has been most satisfactory. The reason for this seems to be that the half court press offense is basically comprised of offensive maneuvers which have already been taught and practiced. These maneuvers are the 3 on 2 fast break situation which develops if a penetrating pass is made into the middle of the defense or the execution of the Regular Zone Offensive pattern if the pass is made to the strongside forward or weakside guard. Both of these situations will have previously been covered with our players in the course of building the fast break and developing our zone offensive package, and they will have been covered in breakdown drills involving two and three players at a time. Therefore, since these kinds of drills have already been practiced, we have never believed that it was necessary to build the half court press offense from a series of drills. Instead we teach from a five on five situation right from the start, confident that our players will be able to recognize the proper offensive maneuvers against the half court press, since these maneuvers are a basic part of our offensive strategy with which they are already familiar.

OFFENSIVE METHODS FOR CONTROLLING
FULL COURT PRESSURE

Throughout the course of a basketball season our team will face more full court pressure than half court pressure. Because of this fact, we have several different ways of dealing with the full court press in its many varieties. We will follow the same basic pattern movements against the full court press, regardless of whether the defense is a man or a zone. The only difference is that we permit more dribbling against the man than against the zone.

I do not believe in merely clearing out the back court against man to man pressure and letting the good ball handler advance the basketball. Certainly I want a good ball handler in possession of the basketball when we are attacking pressure defense, but I do not want that dribbler isolated. He is to always have a teammate behind the line of the basketball as an outlet if the dribbler gets in trouble. Speaking from a defensive viewpoint, we like to see teams clear out against our man to man pressure, and as soon as we see this strategy, our defense will move into a run and jump sequence in which we will trap the basketball in the back court and cut off the immediate passing lanes, which now puts the ball handler in a tough situation. This type of defensive strategy has rewarded us with numerous turnovers. Therefore, when we are on offense, we do not want the same thing happening to our ball handlers. For this reason, in our offense against the full court press, the ball handler knows that there is always a teammate acting as a safety valve receiver if he is needed.

To attack full court pressure, we have three different alignments. Which one is used depends on the opponents and the particular type of defense being used. Although the alignments differ, the principles of the offensive attack remain the same. As with the half court press, we will look for quick penetration with the objective of creating a fast break situation, but if the penetration is not available, then a reversing sequence will be used.

The offense against the full court press is designated as one, three, or four. The number designates the number of immediate in bounds receivers available to the in bounds passer.

THE NUMBER ONE ATTACK

The number one attack sets up in a 1-1-2-1 alignment (Diagram 6–15). Each spot is filled by a designated player, and they are always to align in the designated spot when this offense is being executed. The two guards are down court to put the ball into play, the two forwards are aligned on the back court side of the ten second line, and the high post sets up in the front court near the basket. The players are coached to set up in this alignment before any offensive maneuvers are started. It is the responsibility of the two guards to get the basketball safely in bounds. The in bounds passer is coached to always make sure that he takes the ball out of bounds on one side of the backboard or the other and never to stand directly under the backboard, in order that he can avoid hitting the bottom of the board with an in bounds pass. The other guard, the in bounds receiver, is coached to always line up at the foul line so that he will have fifteen feet of working space to make a move to get open. With these guidelines as a starting point, the offense is now ready to initiate the number one attack.

This offensive series begins with the guard who is in bounds, O2 moving to get open, with an angle cut toward the basketball (Diagram 6–16). This cut, ideally, should be made to the same side of the floor where the in bounds passer, O1, is located. If this is not possible, the cut should be made to the other side of the floor. The point here is that

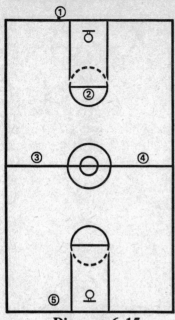

Diagram 6–15

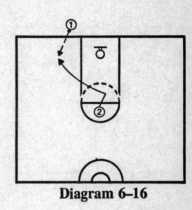

Diagram 6–16

we want the ball to come in bounds on one side of the floor or the other, not in the middle, because we want the offense to establish a strongside and a weakside of the floor.

After the in bounds pass has been made, the in bounds passer, O1, will step in bounds and move to a position on the weakside of the floor near the foul lane and remain a step behind the line of the basketball. At the same time, the weakside forward, O4, will break into the area around the top of the foul circle (Diagram 6–17). When O2 receives the pass, he now becomes the strongside guard, and immediately pivots and reads the defense before doing anything else. One of the key coaching points here is that we do not want any player who receives a pass with his back to the defense to turn and immediately start to dribble. The reason for this coaching point is that we do not want him to pick up a charging foul because he doesn't know the location of the defenders, with a loss of possession resulting. Also, we want this guard to get rid of the basketball immediately if he spots an open man. So on reception of the in bounds pass, we want the receiver to immediately think "read," rather than dribble. The first spot that O2 should read is the foul circle area. O4 will be breaking to this spot, and if he is open,

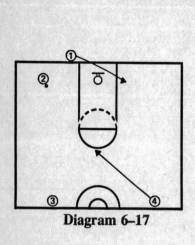

Diagram 6–17

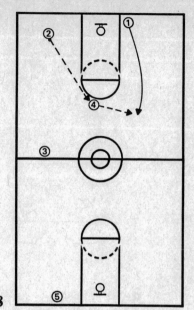

Diagram 6–18

the basketball should be passed to him. When this penetrating pass is made, O1, who has become the weakside guard will break up the sideline, looking for the pass from O4 (Diagram 6–18). These two passes will result in the defense being penetrated and then bypassed before they can recover. With the basketball in the sideline area now, the ball handler will begin dribbling toward the front court. The deep man in the front court, O5, will move over to the ball side corner, and the dribbler will pass into the corner as soon as it is feasible to do so. O4, after dumping the ball off to the side, will fill the middle fast break lane. The other forward, O3, and O1, who passed into the corner, will fill the side lanes, while O2, who originally received the in bounds pass, trails the sequence for floor balance (Diagram 6–19). O5 will read the defense and decide whether the fast break situation exists or not. If the numerical advantage is not present, then the basketball will be returned to the guard, the players will move into their normal positions, and one of the front court offenses will be initiated (Diagram 6–20).

If the defense cuts off the penetrating pass to O4, then the basketball will be returned to O1 after he has set up on the weakside. O4 will clear out of the middle and return to the half court area, and the other

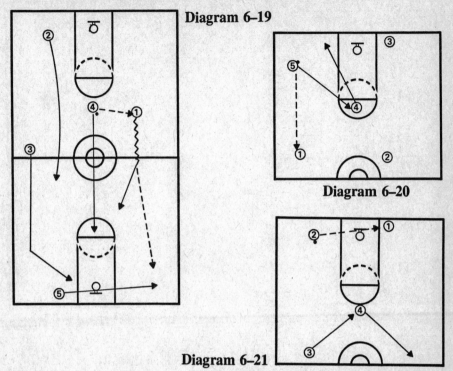

Diagram 6–19

Diagram 6–20

Diagram 6–21

forward, O3, will break into the middle for the penetrating pass (Diagram 6–21). Now the same offensive sequence will be repeated but on the other side of the floor. O2, who received the in bounds pass, will break up the sideline for the quick dump off pass from the middle, and he will dribble the ball toward the front court until the deep man sets up in the corner on the ball side, and then the pass into the front court will be made, with the players filling the fast break lanes as before (Diagram 6–22)

This is the basic sequence we like to follow against the full court press—take time to set up in the proper alignment, be careful to get the basketball in bounds safely, then look for the quick penetrating pass into the middle of the defense and blitz them with a fast break attack.

However, if the quick penetration and the dump out pass are not available because the defense has dropped back to prevent them, then the two guards should be able to handle the press by themselves with a continual reversing of the court with the basketball. The guard with the basketball will dribble up the sideline until challenged, then he will re-

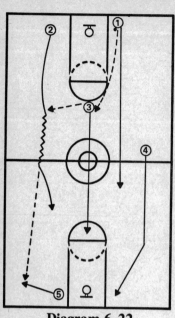

Diagram 6–22

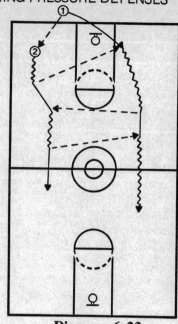

Diagram 6–23

Diagram 6–24

Diagram 6–25

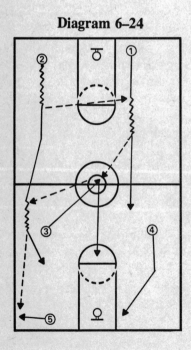

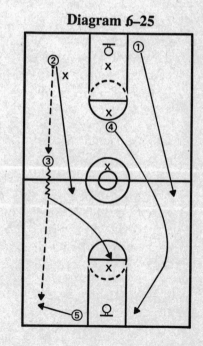

verse the basketball to the other guard, who is a step off the line of the ball on the weakside of the floor. The new ball handler will then begin his dribble toward the sideline or an angle toward the front court until the defense challanges, then he reverses the basketball. This procedure continues until the basketball reaches the front court (Diagram 6–23). This attack will not produce the quick blitz to the basket, but it controls the defense and allows the offense to maneuver into the front court and get into the designated front court offense. As the reversing phase is being executed, the forwards retreat slowly up the floor, keeping the same relative position and distance from the basketball as at the start of the offense. In this situation, the forwards and guards are always reading the defense, and as soon as they recognize that the defense is making a move to deny the reverse pass, then the weakside forward will flash into the middle of the defense, receive a penetrating pass, pivot and read the front court situation and look to dump the ball out to the weakside guard who will be breaking by him, up the sideline. Now with the penetrating pass followed by the dump out pass, even though it has occurred farther up the floor, the blitz attack will procede as usual (Diagram 6–24).

In some cases we have found that the defense is so concerned about denying the pass into the middle that they will forget about the strongside forward. When the strongside guard reads this, he will pass the basketball straight ahead up the floor to the strongside forward who will pivot and read and pass the basketball to the high post in the corner and the fast break lanes will be filled as usual (Diagram 6–25).

One final point about the number one attack. If the in bounds guard is unable to get open to receive the in bounds pass, it is the responsibility of the weakside forward to recognize this predicament and break down the floor so that the basketball can be safely in bounded (Diagram 6–26). Once the ball is in play, the number one attack will be executed as usual. The other forward will break into the middle of the defense for the penetrating pass and when this pass is made, the in bounds guard will break up the sidelines for the dump off pass, and the blitz phase of the offense will be executed (Diagram 6–27). If the penetrating pass is not open, then the two guards and the forward will begin the reverse sequence to move the basketball safely into the front court.

This number one attack works quite well against basic zone and man to man full court pressure. However, when the defense begins to

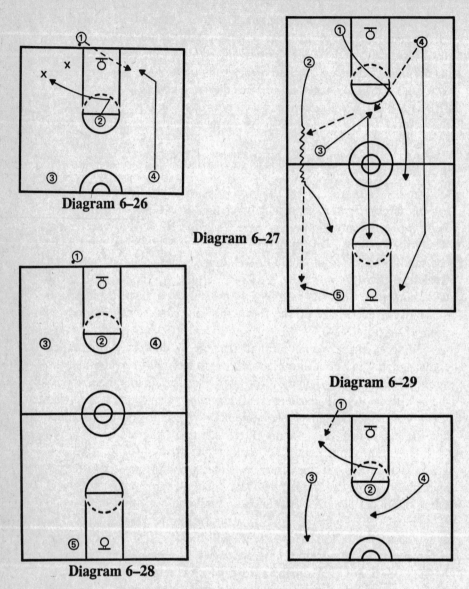

Diagram 6–26

Diagram 6–27

Diagram 6–28

Diagram 6–29

double team the in bounds receiver or puts extreme pressure on the in bounds passer, then we have found it more convenient to align more players in the back court to create more passing lanes to get the ball into play.

THE NUMBER THREE ATTACK

The number three attack aligns the players in a 1-3-1 offensive set (Diagram 6–28). Once again, as in all our alignments against pressure defenses, each player fills his designated position before the offensive attack is started. The starting maneuver for the number three attack is for the guard, O2, who is stationed at the foul line, to make his angle cut to get open. If he gets open and receives the in bounds pass, then O4, who is away from the pass, moves to the middle, O3 on the ball side moves to mid court, and the in bounds passer, O1, moves opposite his pass to the weakside of the floor, a step behind the line of the basketball (Diagram 6–29). O2, in possession of the ball, will turn and read the defense, looking first of all for the penetrating pass into the middle, which will initiate the blitz phase of the offense (Diagram 6–30). If the opportunity to blitz the defense is not available, then the offensive players will maintain a 1-3-1 alignment and advance the basketball up the court by dribbling until challenged, and then passing off. This type of offensive maneuvering will move the ball safely into the front court. If the offense is engaged in the reversing sequence, when the basketball reaches mid court in the sideline area, O5 will break to the ball side corner, the player with the basketball will pass into the corner if this pass is open, and the offense will fill the fast break lanes (Diagram 6–31). Once again, it is the responsibility of O5 to read the defense and make the judgment as to whether the fast break sequence is to be carried through or whether the front court offense should be set up.

If the in bounds pass cannot be made to O2 because of double team pressure, the weakside forward, O4, must move to get open (Diagram 6–32). When this situation occurs, O3 breaks to the middle, O2 breaks up the sideline, and O1 steps in bounds to become the bottom man in the 1-3-1 (Diagram 6–33). O4, after receiving the in bounds pass, will turn and read the defense. If the penetrating pass can be made, then the blitz sequence is carried out. If not, then the reverse sequence will be used to move the basketball into the front court (Diagram 6–34). As the ball is being advanced with the reverse sequence, the offensive player with the basketball must continually be alert to the opportunity to pass the basketball into the middle of the defense. If this can be done, the middle man will look for the dump out pass to the op-

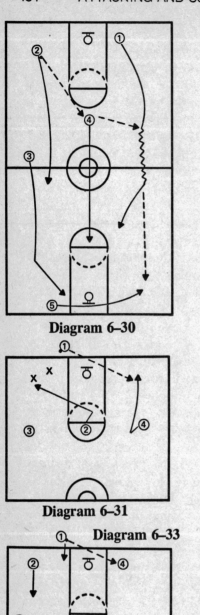

Diagram 6–30

Diagram 6–31

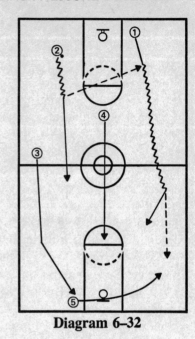

Diagram 6–32

Diagram 6–33

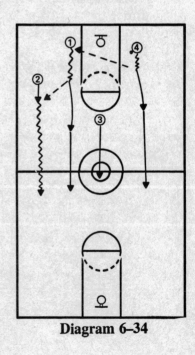

Diagram 6–34

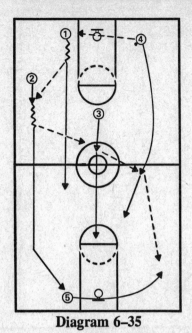

Diagram 6–35

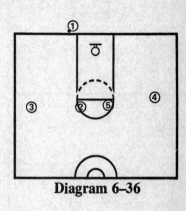

Diagram 6–36

posite sideline. When this is achieved, the basketball will then go to O5 in the corner, and the offense is executed as previously described (Diagram 6–35). If the middle man cannot dump the ball off, he will begin to dribble until he runs into pressure. Then he can move the ball to either side, or to the player behind him, who is trailing the play as an outlet man. The number three attack is not quite as quick hitting as the number one attack, but it provides a relatively secure method of advancing the ball against full court pressure.

THE NUMBER FOUR ATTACK

The third offensive weapon that we use to attack and control full court pressure is the number four attack. We like to use it when we have five good ball handlers or when the defense has a strong and big pressing unit which is pressuring the in bounds passer and aggressively double teaming the basketball when it comes into play. The players set up in designated positions with the alignment resembling a 1-4 offensive set (Diagram 6–36).

The basic pattern is for the in bounds guard, O2, to make his angle cut to get open. When the pass is made to O2, then the forward on the ball side, O3, breaks to mid court. O5 who set up next to O2 in

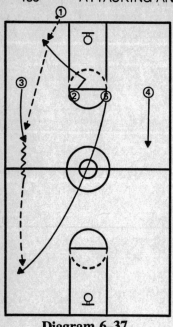

Diagram 6–37

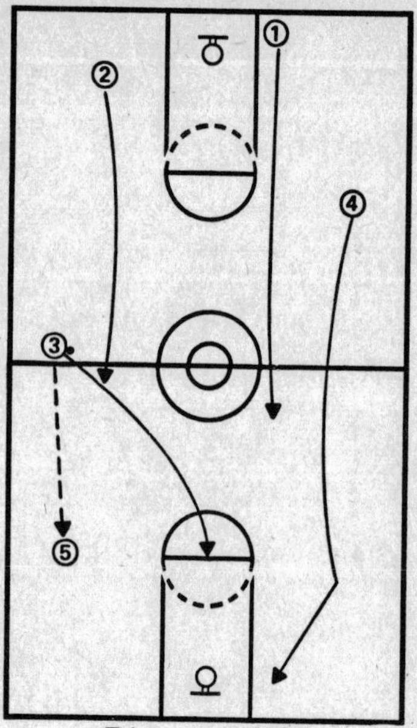

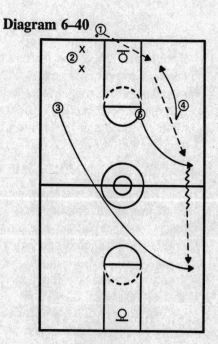

Diagram 6–38

Diagram 6–39

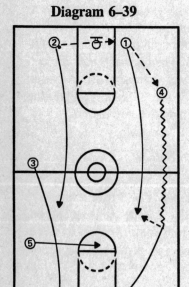

Diagram 6–40

the starting alignment, breaks, on an angle to the front court on the ball side, aiming for a spot at the foul line extended. With these new positions established, O2, who is in possession of the ball, will pivot and read the defense, and, if possible, pass the basketball straight ahead to O3, who in turn will pivot and read and pass to O5 at the foul line extended (Diagram 6–37). If these two passes are made, then the two forwards will fill the other fast break lanes while the two guards trail the play (Diagram 6–38). As always, the offensive player with the basketball in this potential fast break situation reads the defense and makes the decision as to whether the fast break should be continued or whether the front court offense is to be set up.

The primary difference between the number four attack and the other two previously described is that in this offense we are not attempting to penetrate into the middle of the defense. Instead, the idea is to penetrate the outside of the defense by positioning players so that the basketball can be advanced rapidly along the sideline. Therefore, in the number four attack, the weakside forward remains along the sideline away from the basketball, rather than breaking into the middle. This is done because if the ball cannot be immediately thrown up the sideline on the strongside of the floor, it will be returned to the in bounds passer, who has set up as the outlet man, and he will then reverse the ball to the weakside forward on the other sideline, who will usually be able to dribble the balll into the front court and set up the front court offense (Diagram 6–39).

If O2 cannot get open, it is, once again, the responsibility of the weakside forward, O4, to recognize this and move to get open. When the offense is started in this manner, O5 will break ball side to mid court, and O3 will break down into the front court to the foul line extended, and this sets up the sideline penetration sequence once again (Diagram 6–40). When this sequence occurs, O5 is the player who will fill the middle lane, after he makes the pass into the front court, O1 fills the weakside lane, with the other two players trailing the play (Diagram 6–41).

In some cases, the in bounds passer will be able to put the basketball in play with a direct pass to O5 at the foul line. When this entry is made into the offense, both forwards will break down their respective sidelines to the front court, and O5 will hit either player if they get open, and then he will fill the middle lane. If the forwards do not get open, both guards are behind the line of the basketball for a pass to start the reversing process (Diagram 6–42).

INSTALLING THE FULL COURT PRESS OFFENSE

Our full court press offense is developed through the same stages as the half court press offense. First the total offensive strategy is explained and demonstrated. Then the players walk through the various offensive maneuvers to develop a total understanding of the offense. Next the offense is run at full speed, but without a defense, and finally, it is executed against all the varieties of the full court presses.

As with the half court press offense, we have no specific drills, because after we get the basketball into play, we immediately try to establish a fast break situation into the front court. So, in effect, when we are working on our fast break drills, we are at the same time drilling our players to handle the pressing situation, as well. By constant repetition of five on five full court work, the players can develop the poise and reading ability which are needed to make the proper judgments for attacking and controlling full court pressure.

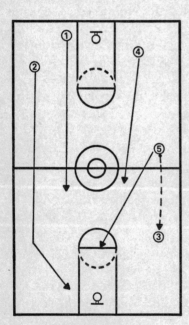

Diagram 6–41

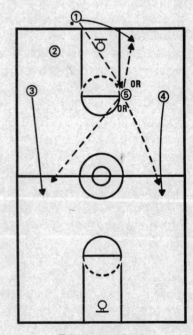

Diagram 6–42

The ultimate test of a player's poise is his ability to exhibit proper mental and physical control against the full court press. He must learn what kinds of passes to use and what kinds not to use; he must learn when to take advantage of the quick scoring opportunity and when to set up the front court offense. All of this can be developed if the players are taught a definite set of principles and player alignments which will permit the carrying out of those principles. These things must then be practiced enough so that the players can move into such an attack when necessary with utmost confidence. As with all coaching situations, the coach must be patient as the players learn how to attack and control pressure defenses. This phase of the offensive system must be installed early enough in the pre-season practice so that the players will have enough practice time to develop proper understanding of the offense. As this understanding develops, so, too, will the necessary poise and judgment which are needed to make the offense an effective weapon for attacking and controlling the defense.

The offense which is confident of its capability to attack pressure defenses will take away another method by which the defense tries to control things. Once again, a simple, but flexible approach which is based on sound principles and then practiced until it becomes an automatic reaction will give the offense yet another means of establishing and maintaining court control and will result in the defense, rather than the offense, being placed under constant pressure.

7

PREPARING FOR
SPECIAL SITUATIONS

Although basketball games are generally a contest between basic front court offenses and basic front court defenses, throughout the course of every game, special situations arise which require special strategy and tactics. These special situations may ultimately decide the outcome of any given game. Therefore, in order to be as totally prepared as possible to play a basketball game, a team must have definite plans to follow when faced with special situations. These plans must be given adequate practice time so that there will be proper understanding and timing when a team is called on to use the special maneuvers.

ATTACKING COMBINATION DEFENSES

Facing combination defenses has been the exception rather than the rule for our basketball teams. Possibly this is due to the fact that our offensive system is designed to try and produce offensive balance to force the defense to be concerned with all five players. However, there have been occasions when our opponents have used combination defenses against particular individuals. Since the combination defense is the exception, we believe that the best way for us to attack it is by using one of the offensive patterns with which players are already familiar. Sometimes we can position the players in such a way that the pattern can be executed in its usual way. At other times we will make a minor adjustment here or there in one of the basic patterns. Regardless, we have found that this has worked well for us since player familiarity with a particular pattern leads to a more confident execution.

THE OFFENSE VS THE BOX AND ONE

In attacking the Box and One Defense, we have two offensive series. The first series places the individual who is being guarded man to man, O5, in the high post position. The Overload Zone Offense is then executed. O5 will break to either corner, with the low post player screening O5's defender as he makes his cut (Diagram 7–1). As in the Regular Overload Offense, the screener, O3, will turn toward the basketball after screening, looking for the pass if the defense forgets him. O1 will read the defense and get the basketball to the open man, either the player in the corner or the strongside low post or to O2 who circles in behind the defense to the foul line.

If the pass is made to the corner, but no shot is available, the basketball will then be reversed as usual, but with one minor adjustment against the man to man coverage on the corner player. The ball will be returned to O1, and O2 will return to his starting position and receive a pass. He will then pass into the wing area to O4, as the two post players make the usual reverse phase move of the Overload Offense (Diagram 7–2). At this point of the offense the minor adjustment takes place. O1, who is now the weakside guard, breaks inside and sets a vertical, head hunting screen on the defensive player, who is playing man to man. O5 will then break off the screen to the foul circle, looking for the pass and possible jump shot. This move now gives O4 the chance to post the basketball either high or low (Diagram 7–3). If no shot develops from this sequence of moves, then the basketball is moved back out on top, the screening guard returns to his starting position, the forwards move into their post spots, and the offense is ready to start the same cycle over again (Diagram 7–4).

The second series we use to attack the Box and One Defense places the player being guarded man to man in one of the forward positions. We will then start the offense away from him and run the Oppo-

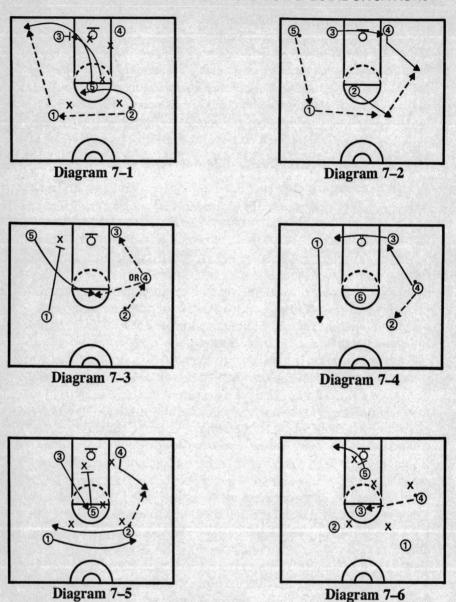

Diagram 7–1

Diagram 7–2

Diagram 7–3

Diagram 7–4

Diagram 7–5

Diagram 7–6

site adjustment of the Regular Zone Offense. The only change is that O5 will set a head hunting screen on the man to man defender as he rolls opposite the basketball (Diagram 7–5). One of two situations should be looked for as a result of this maneuver. First, O3, being guarded man to man, will break open for the jump shot at the foul line (Diagram 7–6). Second, the defender who is playing zone in the vicinity of the high post will decide to help his teammate out when he is screened and will let O5 go, with the result that O5 will be wide open underneath, since the man to man defender will be trying to avoid his screen and defend the cut to the foul line (Diagram 7–7). If neither of these possibilities occur, then the offense will reverse the basketball and try to post it, just as is done in the Opposite Adjustment of the Regular Zone Offense (Diagram 7–8). If no shot has developed by this time, the basketball will be returned to the top of the floor, O3, being guarded man to man will remain in the high post position, and the offense will then run the Overload Attack for a combination defense as just described (Diagram 7–9).

THE OFFENSE VS THE TRIANGLE AND TWO

Another combination defense which could be faced is the triangle and two. If presented with this kind of defense, in which two of our players are being guarded man to man, we would place them in the two guard spots, forcing the defense into a coverage in which the top of the defense is man and the bottom of the defense is zone. This position adjustment now gives us two offenses, one to attack the triangle and two and one with which to attack a combination in which the top of the defense is man and the bottom of the defense is zone.

In this offensive set, we would run the Regular Zone Offense, with a slight adjustment. As previously described in Chapter 3, when the entry pass is made to the strongside forward, the high post rolls low on the ball side, and the two guards cross and change floor positions.

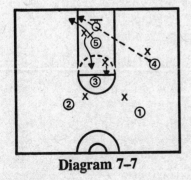

Diagram 7–7

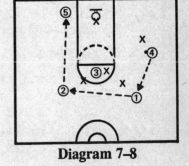

Diagram 7–8

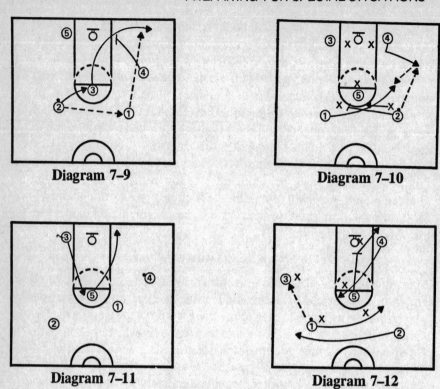

Diagram 7–9

Diagram 7–10

Diagram 7–11

Diagram 7–12

When facing the triangle and two, the same entry maneuver is executed, with the adjustment that when the two guards begin their crossing maneuver, the strongside guard, O2, will screen for the weakside guard, O1 to try and free him for an open jump shot at the edge of the foul circle (Diagram 7–10). The rest of the offense then continues as usual against the zone, with the weakside forward flashing high (Diagram 7–11). If no shot develops from this phase of the offense, then the reverse phase of the offense is executed as described in Chapter 3.

THE OFFENSE VS TOP ZONE, BOTTOM MAN

If faced with a combination defense in which the top of the defense is a zone while the bottom of the defense is man to man, the offense would be instructed to run the Opposite Adjustment of the Regular Zone Offense. The adjustment which would be made to the normal pattern would be the same adjustment used against the Box and One Defense. When O5 rolls opposite the entry pass, he will set a head hunting screen for the weakside forward (Diagram 7–12). If a penetrating pass can be made to the foul circle, then a good percentage jump shot will be produced. If not, then the basketball will be reversed and posted if at all possible (Diagram 7–13). This part of the offense is usually very effective because of the defensive sag on the weakside, which puts that defender in a position which makes it difficult for him to establish a denial position on the post man when the basketball is reversed. If no shot develops, then the players remain in their new positions, and the offensive sequence will be run again.

These four combination defenses are the types which our basketball teams have confronted at one time or another over the years. As can be readily seen from the description of the various offensive maneuvers, our primary strategy against the combination defense is to utilize an offensive pattern with which our players are already familiar. With these basic patterns we then add minor adjustments which specifically take advantage of the type of combination defense being faced.

ATTACKING MATCH UP DEFENSES

In today's basketball, Match Up Defenses are becoming more and more popular because coaches are finding that the Match Up Defense combines the strengths of both the man to man and zone defenses. Thus, the Match Up Defense can provide pressure on the basketball and denial of immediate passing lanes, which is characteristic of the man to man, while at the same time assuring defensive help by using the basic zone principles away from the basketball.

In attacking a match up defense we force the defense to be concerned with cutters. We want the defense to cover cutters who are mov-

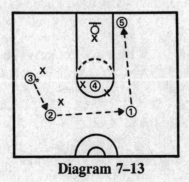

Diagram 7–13

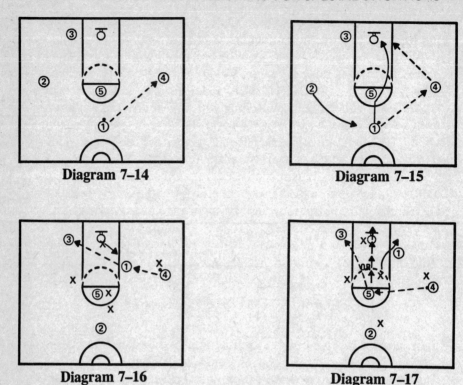

Diagram 7–14

Diagram 7–15

Diagram 7–16

Diagram 7–17

ing from weakside to strongside floor positions trying to force defensive errors in coverage. Basically, we are trying to maneuver the match up defense into a situation which forces them to play our pattern man to man.

We have two offensive attacks to use against the match up. The first offense is the Overload Offense as described in Chapter 4. The Overload Offense gives the offense the opportunity to move a cutter through the defense and break him into the corner by use of screens, putting him in position for the high percentage shot. While this entry move is underway, the weakside guard cuts into the foul circle area, looking for the possible penetrating pass there. The offensive players read and execute the Overload Offense just as if they were attacking a zone defense. We have found that our players' familiarity with the pattern results in the Overload Offense being an effective offense against the match up. Both the strongside and reverse phases of the offense contain maneuvers which are effective against both a man or a zone defense, and so the Overload seems tailor made for use against a match up defense.

THE 1-3-1 MATCH UP OFFENSE

We have one special offensive pattern which is specifically designed for use against a match up defense. This pattern is executed from a 1-3-1 alignment. We have found that by establishing a 1-3-1 set, the defense will match up into a 1-3-1, and then we use a series of cutting and screening options to pressure the defense and produce high percentage shots. To start this offense, the entry pass is made to the wing area away from the low post (Diagram 7–14). Once the entry pass is made, the 1-3-1 Match Up Offense moves through four options.

1st Option—Give and Go—As soon as the point man, O1, makes his pass to O4, he will cut off the high post, down the lane, looking for the quick return pass. O2 will rotate out on top as this first option is carried out (Diagram 7–15). This give and go maneuver forces the defense to deal with a cutter who is breaking into the center of the defense, and if he is not covered, the defense will be penetrated and the lay up will result. If the lane defenders switch the cutter as he moves through the lane, the ball can often be passed inside and as the low defender moves to cover the point man, he can dump the ball off to his teammate, O3, in the low post before the weakside defender can deny the pass (Diagram 7–16). If the high post defender slides down the lane with the cutter, then O5 will be open at the foul line for the jump shot or be able to throw a quick pass into the low post (Diagram 7–17). Regardless of what happens, the defense is forced to adjust and adjust quickly, or they will be victimized by a high percentage shot. If the defense is able to cut off the quick penetrating option, then the offense moves into the second option.

2nd Option—Screen for Low Post—After O1 has made his cut down the lane and realized he will not receive a pass, he will then move across the foul lane and set a screen on the defender who is responsible for the low post area, and O3 will break across the lane looking for the pass in the lane area, or after he sets up in the strongside low post (Diagram 7–18). O1, after screening, remains in the weakside low post.

3rd Option—High Post Roll—If O3 does not receive a pass, he

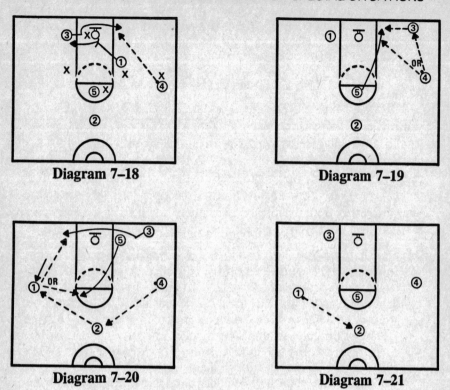

Diagram 7–18

Diagram 7–19

Diagram 7–20

Diagram 7–21

will move half way to the corner, and O5 will roll down the lane, on the ball side, and set up in the strongside low post. The ball can then be passed in, either from the wing, or it can be moved into the corner, where O3, who set up there, will have the short jump shot if not covered, or if covered, will be able to post the basketball (Diagram 7–19).

4th Option—Reverse—If no scoring opportunity has developed by this time, the basketball will be reversed to the other side of the floor to O1, who moves to the wing area on the other side of the floor to receive a pass. As the basketball reaches the wing area on the other side of the floor, O3 will break off a screen set by O5 in the low post and establish a position in the ball side low post. O5, after the cutter has made his move, will flash to the high post area (Diagram 7–20). These moves give the offense another chance at penetration into the post areas. However, if no shot results, the offense, with these last two moves, has reset itself in the 1-3-1 alignment with only O1 and O2 having changed floor positions. The Match Up Offense is now ready to start again. (Diagram 7–21).

These two offensive attacks, the Overload and the 1-3-1, have proved quite adequate for use against the Match Up Defense. They have proved successful because they tend to spread the defense out, resulting in more floor space having to be defended, which means less chance for defensive help, and more concern on the part of the defense to use man to man principles. This factor then enables the offense to attack with the various cuts and screens which will result in high percentage scoring attempts against the Match Up Defense.

JUMP BALL SITUATIONS

Since our basketball philosophy is based on the principle of control, we follow the same theory in regard to the jump ball. Controlling the situation on the jump ball means that we will either try to ensure ourselves of possession of the basketball, or if we believe that possession is doubtful, set up so that we can control the opponents when they gain possession.

The jump ball, for strategic purposes, is divided into three situations: even (control uncertain); us (control assured); them (control not possible). For the even and us situations, the players will align themselves so that there is always an open spot on the circle, that is, an area where we will have two players positioned with no defender between them (Diagram 7–22). Our jumper must find the open spot and tip the basketball to that area. Our two players at the open spot are to screen the player next to them to prevent a crashing of the open spot. If we have established an open spot so will our opponents, but if the situation is us we don't care. If the situation is even we will crash the opponents' open spot as soon as the ball is touched by the jumpers. If the jump situation is them, our players will align in a defensive set up so that although we will not gain possession, we will be in position to control the opponents' offense and make them set up rather than giving up a quick score. This means that we will usually place three players toward the opponents' offensive end of the court (Diagram 7–23).

If an opponent has definite types of plays from jump ball situations, we will either position or maneuver players in a manner designed to either intercept the tip or a pass after possession or upset the timing

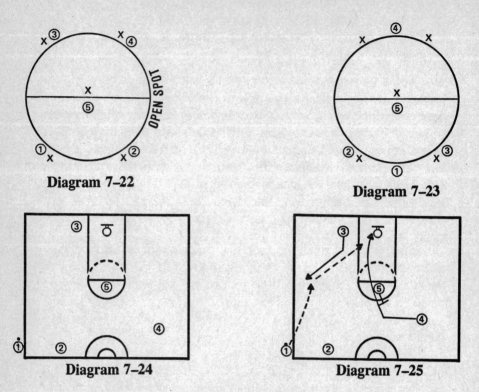

Diagram 7–22

Diagram 7–23

Diagram 7–24

Diagram 7–25

of the maneuver to deny the preplanned play.

The principle of control is all that we are concerned with in regard to the jump ball situation. If we gain possession and a quick scoring opportunity is available, our players are expected to take advantage of it. However, we do not have any specific scoring plays from the jump ball situation. The primary concern is control of the basketball or control of the situation.

OUT OF BOUNDS SITUATIONS

The out of bounds situation occurs often enough in the course of a basketball game to warrant special offensive consideration. We regard these situations as excellent opportunities to initiate offensive sequences designed to produce the high percentage shot. We will try to execute special offensive maneuvers from the sideline out of bounds whenever the defense is man to man and from the baseline, everytime, regardless of the type of defense.

SIDELINE OUT OF BOUNDS

When the basketball is put into play from the front court sideline, if the front court defense is a zone, then we will simply pass the ball in bounds and attack the defense with one of the front court zone offenses. However, if the defense is man to man, the offense will try to create an immediate scoring opportunity. Our sideline out of bounds offense has three different scoring maneuvers. All three are run from the same alignment (Diagram 7–24). The designated guard takes the ball out of bounds, while the other guard sets up near the mid court line. The high post and the strongside forward set up in their normal 2-1-2 positions, and the weakside forward moves out to the weakside guard spot. From this alignment we are now ready to run one of three maneuvers: the sneak cut, the low post, or the quick screen.

Sneak Cut—The in bound passer, O1, will slap the basketball as the signal to begin the offensive action. On the slap of the basketball, O3 will make his ninety degree cut to get open at the foul line extended to receive the in bounds pass. As the basketball is put into play, O4 will move to the middle of the floor and then make a quick cut off a screen set by O5 (Diagram 7–25), looking for the pass for a lay up.

If the scoring pass cannot be thrown to the cutting forward, he simply continues across the lane and sets up in his normal position, the basketball goes back out on top to O1, and the 2-1-2 alignment is set up to begin their attack (Diagram 7–26).

If the basketball cannot be in bounded to O3, it is the responsibility of O5 and O2 to maneuver to get open, and the ball will be in bounded to either of these players (Diagram 7–27). If the pass is made to O5, O3 will cut to the basket looking for the quick pass. If the basketball is passed into O2, or if O5 cannot hit the cutting forward, then the players move into the 2-1-2 set and run the designated front court offense.

Low Post—For the low post sequence, the player alignment is the same, and the entry pass is as previously described. The difference in this sequence is that as the pass is in bounded, O4 moves to the middle of the floor, and O5 takes one step up as if to set a screen, but then pivots and rolls down the lane, looking for a pass from O3 (Diagram 7–28).

If the basketball cannot be passed to the cutter, it is passed back

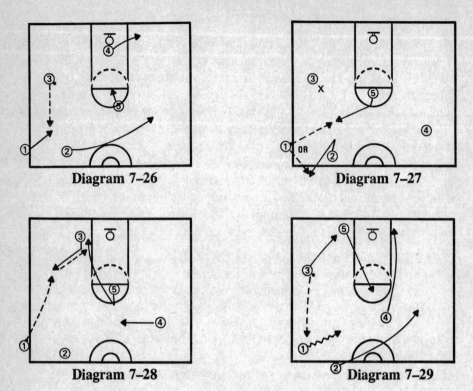

Diagram 7–26   Diagram 7–27

Diagram 7–28   Diagram 7–29

out on top and the offense sets up in its 2-1-2 (Diagram 7–29). If the ball cannot be in bounded to O3, again it is the responsibility of O5 and O2 to get open for the in bounds pass and the offense will follow the same procedure as described above.

Quick Screen—This is the final out of bounds play from the sideline against the man to man defense. The alignment is the same as for the other two plays, and O3 makes his normal move to get open. However, the basketball will be inbounded this time to O2. The basketball is reversed to O4, and he will look for the in bound passer, O1, who after in bounding the basketball, will break off a screen set by O3 and cut across the lane area (Diagram 7–30). If the pass underneath cannot be made, the basketball is returned to O2 on the top of the floor, and the players set up in the 2-1-2 alignment (Diagram 7–31). In case of difficulty getting the ball in bounds to O2, O5 must move to get open, and when he receives the pass, he will look for the breaking O3, and if he is not open, the usual alignment will be established.

The sideline out of bounds plays give the offense another offensive weapon with which to attack the defense, another manner of trying to achieve a quick scoring maneuver and a high percentage shot from a situation which is usually not regarded as a scoring situation. But in trying to achieve the concept of court control, no opportunity should be overlooked in attacking and destroying the confidence of the defense.

BASELINE OUT OF BOUNDS

Regardless of the type of defense used by our opponents on the baseline out of bounds situation, we will execute some type of offensive maneuver designed to free a player for the high percentage shot. The offensive alignment on the baseline is a box formation (Diagram 7–32). From this alignment we have one offensive series for attacking the man to man defense and one series to use against the zone. One player, usually the high post, is designated as the in bounds passer and will call which sequence is to be used.

OFFENSIVE SERIES VS THE MAN TO MAN

When the in bounds passer, O5, has identified the defense for the other players, he will then slap the basketball as a signal to start the offense. On the signal, the low man on the ball side, O4, will break out toward the corner with his hands raised, calling for the basketball. This maneuver is designed to attract the attention of the defense. At the same time, O3 in the low post away from the basketball, breaks across the lane to the opposite side of the foul circle and sets a head hunting screen for O2 on the ball side of the floor. O2 must wait for the screen and then break over it to the basket (Diagram 7–33). After O2 has cut

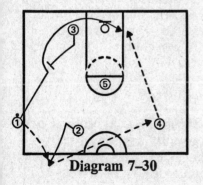

Diagram 7–30

Diagram 7–31

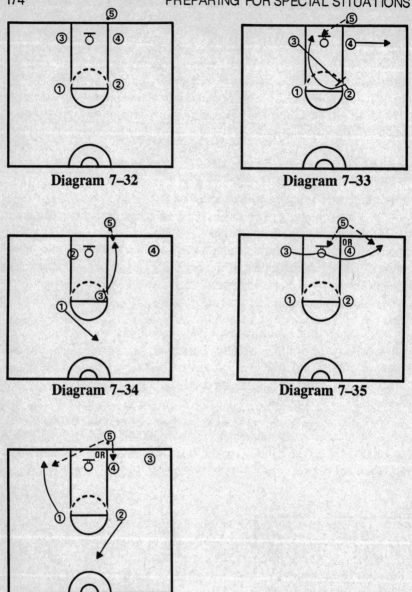

Diagram 7–32

Diagram 7–33

Diagram 7–34

Diagram 7–35

Diagram 7–36

off the screen, O3 will roll down the lane, while O1 backs off for floor balance (Diagram 7–34). These two cuts give the in bound passer two opportunities to get the ball inside for the lay up. If neither cutter is open, the basketball will be in bounded either to O4 in the corner or O2, and the designated half court offense will be set up.

OFFENSIVE SERIES VS THE ZONE

If the baseline defense is identified as a zone, the same box formation is used, but the offensive maneuvers are altered. Once again, the in bound passer, O5, will identify the defense and slap the basketball. On the signal, the low man away from the ball, O3, will break across the lane, hesitate in the middle of the lane for a possible quick pass, but when not receiving such a pass will continue across the lane, breaking off a screen set by the low man on the ball side, O4, and move half way to the corner for the in bound pass and the open jump shot (Diagram 7–35). Also, on the signal, the guard away from the ball, O1, breaks to the corner on his side of the floor, and becomes the second pass receiver for the in bounds passer, while O2 on the ball side moves out for floor balance, and O4 on the ball side remains in the low post for a quick inside pass if the defense forgets him (Diagram 7–36). After passing the ball in bounds against the zone defense, O5 will always go to the open post area. By doing this, he will be on the weakside to rebound if he passes into O3, or he will be set up in the strongside low post if he passes into O1. If the open shot is not produced, then the designated front court offense is set up.

These two baseline series are very simple to execute and we have had very good results using these maneuvers year after year in obtaining high percentage shots. The baseline out of bounds plays represent another weapon in our offensive arsenal by which we establish court control.

EMERGENCY SCORE SITUATIONS

The emergency score situation is not an every game happening. It is a highly specialized situation which a team will usually face only one or two times a season, but when faced with it, a definite approach to the situation is necessary to deal successfully with the emergency. The emergency score situation exists when the offense is faced with the task of scoring in the last ten seconds of the basketball game. It is a situation in which, if a team is to be totally prepared, they must be able to execute some kind of offensive maneuver which will produce a shot opportunity which will win or tie the game.

Our emergency score plays are divided into full court, back court, and mid court. The maneuvers are designed to be run in basically the same way regardless of the location and regardless of whether the defense is man to man or zone. In an emergency situation we will not have time to differentiate between defenses. Therefore, what we try to do is develop the proper timing of the offensive maneuvers so that our best outside shooter will be able to break off a double screen, receive an accurate pass, and fire away at the basket. These emergency score plays are designed to be used when there are ten seconds or less left in the game and we need a basket to either tie or win. If there are more than ten seconds left, then we will run a designated option of one of our front court offenses.

How we will run the emergency score play will also depend on how much time is on the clock. If there are more than five seconds, we will in bound the basketball to a designated player and he will pass to our emergency scorer. This process is followed to cut down on the distance the ball will have to travel in the air. However, if there are five seconds or less left, then the basketball will be passed to our emergency scorer from out of bounds.

FULL COURT PLAY

The alignment for the full court play has the emergency scorer, O3, lined up in the low post on the opposite side of the basketball, while two strong rebounders line up on the other side of the lane, O4 in the low post area, O5 just below the foul line, with the remaining two players used for advancing the basketball. If there are more than five seconds on the clock, the pass will be in bounded to O2. He will have tried to line up as near to mid court as possible to cut down on the distances of the passes. On the reception of the pass he will immediately pivot and throw the basketball into the corner where O3 will have broken to off a double screen set by his teammates in the front court (Diagram 7–37). The emergency scorer is coached to start his break across the lane when the basketball leaves the in bound passer's hands. We work on players throwing the basketball into the corner at chest or chin level, so that the emergency scorer can catch the ball in the shooting position, turn, and fire away.

If there are five seconds or less remaining, then the basketball will be thrown the length of the court from out of bounds. It is an obvious coaching point that you must find one, or hopefully, two players on your team who have the ability to throw the length of the court pass strongly and accurately, and then make sure that they have the opportunity to practice this skill each week. In this situation, with the basketball having to travel the length of the court, the immediate in bounds pass receiver, O2, will line up away from the in bound passer to draw the defense away from the basketball. The emergency scorer will break across the lane, off the double screen and into the ball side corner as soon as the official hands the in bound passer the basketball. The pass is to be thrown immediately, so that the five second violation can be avoided, since the ball must travel the length of the court while the count is on (Diagram 7–38).

This basic offensive maneuver is used regardless of whether the defense is in a man to man or a zone. It is up to the screeners to read the type of defense and carry out the proper screen. If the defense is man to man, then the screeners will set up in a double screen and pick off the emergency scorer's man. If the defense is a zone, then the screeners will set single screens on the two defenders closest to the shooting corner.

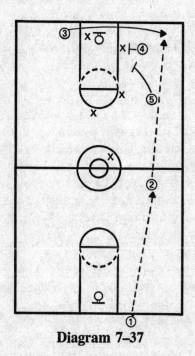

Diagram 7–37

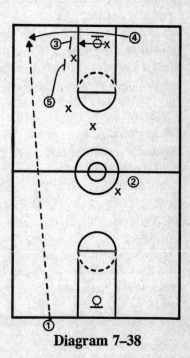

Diagram 7–38

When the shot is taken, the players will move to designated re-bound spots. O5, who is the highest on the floor, will rebound the weakside; O3, lowest on the floor, will rebound on the side from where the shot is taken, O2 who was the in-bound pass receiver will break to the middle rebound spot, and the shooter will follow his shot (Diagram 7–39).

BACK COURT PLAY

The back court emergency score play is used when we have pos-session of the basketball and it is to be put into play at the foul line ex-tended in the back court. The play is executed the same as the full court play. If there are more than five seconds, the basketball will be in bounded to a guard who will then pass it into the corner to the emergency scorer, who in this situation will wait until the ball is in bounded and then break to the corner off the double screen, with the screeners either picking off their men or walling off the zone defense (Diagram 7–40).

If there are five seconds or less, then the pass goes directly to the emergency scorer from out of bounds. As previously stated, the emergency scorer breaks for the opposite corner as soon as the official hands the ball to the in bound passer, who immediately passes the bas-ketball into the corner (Diagram 7–41). The rebounding positions are filled as previously stated in the full court play.

FRONT COURT PLAY

If we have possession at either mid-court or the front court foul line extended, the front court play will be used. The only difference be-tween the front court play and the other two emergency score plays is that the basketball will always be thrown directly to the emergency scorer as he breaks off the double screen. Once again he will start his break as soon as the official hands the in-bound passer the basketball, cut off the screen, catch the basketball, and fire away (Diagram 7–42). The rebounding spots are covered the same as with the other two emergency score plays.

If we would have possession of the basketball on the baseline in a ten second or less situation, we would simply run one of our baseline out of bounds plays.

These emergency score plays are basically very simple, but we

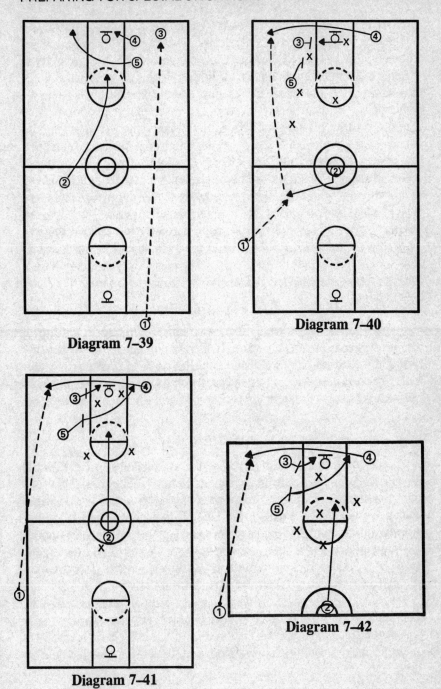

Diagram 7–39

Diagram 7–40

Diagram 7–41

Diagram 7–42

feel that this simplicity is necessary since the time factor prevents a maneuver which is complex and time consuming. Then, too, since these types of plays are used so seldom, not as much multiplicity is needed. The most important factor in the success of these plays is the proper timing of the break, the screens, and the pass, so that as with the other phases of the offensive system, the coach must be willing to find the time within his practice sequence to make sure that these fundamentals are developed to ensure proper execution. We have found that the strategy of the double screen works equally well against any kind of defense when it is set on the perimeter of the defense, allowing the good shooter to get the open outside shot. These emergency score plays, while a small part of the overall offensive system, should not be neglected. When the situation arises, the emergency score plays will give you the opportunity of securing the open shot while at the same time creating the feeling in the minds of your players that they have a definite plan of attack for just such a situation.

THE DELAY GAME

No flexible offensive system is complete without some form of the delay game. The delay game is merely another means at the disposal of the offense for establishing and maintaining court control. Our delay game is divided into three phases: control, stall, and freeze. Each phase represents a different approach to controlling the offensive situation.

CONTROL

The control phase of the delay game runs time off the clock, while not passing up a high percentage shot opportunity. The control phase is run from the Regular man to man front court pattern, with the weakside guard always cutting through the lane. It is executed by having the players run through the Regular man to man pattern to the third option, the vertical screen for the weakside forward. When running the control, the weakside forward moves off the screen and will go as high on the floor as necessary to receive a pass from the strongside forward. After receiving this pass, the weakside forward will return the basketball to the guard who made the first cut and will now be returning to the top of the floor. The players now return to the 2-1-2 alignment, with only the guards having changed floor positions (Diagram 7–43). The same offensive sequence is run again, with the basketball passed from the strongside forward to the weakside forward as he breaks off the vertical screen. Once again, the ball is returned to the guard. Now the pattern is repeated for the third time, but now as the pattern is being executed, the offense is looking for the high percentage shot. If no shot develops, the offense continues to hold the basketball and run the Regular man to man pattern until a good scoring opportunity is presented.

When the offense goes through the first two sequences of the control, the strongside forward is instructed to pass the basketball to the cutting guards, only if either one breaks free and is open for the lay up shot. Other than the lay up, no shots are to be taken during the first two sequences of the control.

The control phase of our delay game allows us to wind time off the clock while staying with one of our basic patterns. This enables us to run time off the clock while the defense is under the impression that they are doing a good job, when in fact, the offense is in total control of the front court situation.

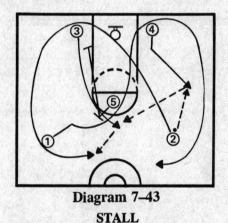

Diagram 7–43

STALL

The stall phase of the delay game takes us out of our normal offensive alignment and has as its objective keeping control of the basketball until an uncontested lay up is possible. Thus the stall is a lay up only offense, and all other shots are to be passed up. The stall operates from a spread out 3-2 alignment and moves through a series of four options aimed at keeping the defense busy, so they cannot two-time the basketball, and create lay up opportunities for the offense.

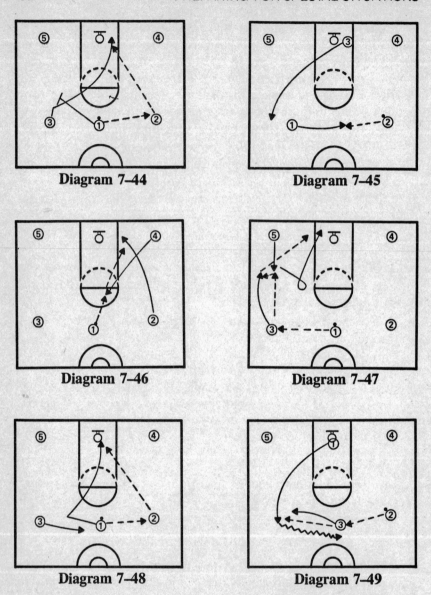

Diagram 7-44

Diagram 7-45

Diagram 7-46

Diagram 7-47

Diagram 7-48

Diagram 7-49

1st Option—*Screen Opposite*—The stall sequence begins with
O1 passing to one of the wing men, O2. O1 then breaks opposite
his pass and sets a screen for the weakside wing man, O3, breaks
off the screen, down the lane, looking for the pass for the lay up
(Diagram 7-44). If no pass is made, O3 continues back out to the

floor position he originally occupied, and O1 moves back to the middle of the floor and gets the basketball back (Diagram 7–45).

2nd Option—*Corner Backdoor*—The second option now is initiated on the same side of the floor to which the basketball was first passed. As soon as O2 returns the ball to O1, the corner man, O4, on the original strongside of the floor breaks to the foul circle. The point man passes into the foul circle and, as this pass is being made, the wing man on that side, O2. breaks to the basket looking for the backdoor pass (Diagram 7–46). If the backdoor option does not result in a lay up, the players return to their original floor positions.

3rd Option—*Bonnie Cut*—If the corner backdoor option has not produced a shot, the basketball is returned to O1, and he moves the basketball to the other wing man, O3. The corner man, O5, on the ball side of the floor fakes toward the basket and then moves out to the foul line extended to receive a pass from O3. O3 follows his pass, receiving the basketball back from O5, who then executes a bonnie cut to the basket (Diagram 7–47). If the ball cannot be passed inside, O1 moves to get the basketball, and the players re-establish their 3-2 alignment.

4th Option—*Change Up*—The final option in the stall sequence is the change-up option. It is executed to give the appearance of starting the entire pattern over again. O1 starts the option by passing to one of the wing men, and begins to cut opposite his pass, but, instead of setting a screen, he changes direction after several steps and breaks down the lane looking for the pass for the lay up shot (Diagram 7–48). If O1 does not receive a pass, O3 breaks to the middle of the floor and receives the basketball. O1 returns to the top of the floor, receives the basketball, and the team then resets in the 3-2 alignment (Diagram 7–49). With the stall alignment reset, the entire stall sequence starts again.

FREEZE

The Freeze phase of the Delay Game is used when we are interested totally in running time off the clock while maintaining possession of the basketball. The freeze is our "save the game" offense in which we are not interested in scoring, but with keeping away from the opponents. No shots are to be taken when we are in the freeze. The player alignment is the same wide 3-2 set up as used in the stall, but there is no definite pattern which is executed. Instead, the freeze is carried out by following a set of rules. The rules for the Freeze are as follows:

1. Keep the basketball moving, using passes more than the dribble.
2. Players without the basketball must always make angle cuts to get open.
3. Players without the basketball are not to cross on the basketball, as this creates trapping opportunity for the defense, so stay away from the basketball.
4. Do not give up the dribble, save it for when it is needed.
5. Avoid trapping situations by passing the basketball before the defense can set the trap.
6. Avoid drawing an offensive foul.
7. Take a five second count rather than throwing a bad pass.
8. Expect a lot of physical contact from the defense.

Keeping these rules in mind, we simply tell the offense to play keep away. The freeze is practiced on a half court basis once a week during the season. This type of approach has provided an effective attack when possession of the basketball is more important than points.

These special situations are a most important phase of the concept of court control basketball. If the concept of court control is to be an actuality, then preparation to handle the special situations is a must. A definite plan of action in regard to the special situations, one in which adequate practice time is spent so that proper understanding, execution and timing are achieved, will create a sense of court control in the minds of both players and coaches. This feeling will develop because all concerned will be aware that no matter what type of special offensive situation might arise, the offensive arsenal will have something available which has been practiced and then stored away for use in the special situation.

The awareness on the part of the players that they have been prepared to meet a variety of situations is the strong foundation on which full court control basketball is built. This knowledge of preparation to handle special situations helps develop the poise which is so necessary for success. The poise created by preparation leads to mental control among the players, and the mental control having been established, means that physical control of the situation has a much better chance of being achieved. It is from such preparation that the concept of full court control becomes a reality.

8

EVALUATING INDIVIDUAL
AND TEAM PERFORMANCE

PURPOSE OF EVALUATION

In any type of endeavor in which the end result is of prime importance, some form of evaluation is a necessity to indicate what is being achieved or what progress is being made toward achievement. I am sure that all coaches are interested in knowing both the strengths and weaknesses of their basketball teams, on both an individual and a team basis. I do not think that any coach, simply sitting on the bench and watching the game progress is the answer. All coaches can see what the opponents are doing and make adjustments according to their game style, and they are aware of which players are playing well or below par and take necessary action. However, there are very few coaches who have the ability to accurately evaluate a total picture of both individual and team performance after the game is over, by mere recall. Certain plays and players will stick in the coach's mind, but a total overview is not possible without some form of evaluation.

To achieve as complete an evaluation as possible, we use two specific methods in which both individual and team performances are charted. These charts are then reviewed after the game, transferred to a master chart, and then graded. The grade can then be compared with previous standards to indicate performance, and the range of grades will be an indication as to the adequacies or deficiencies in a particular game.

In order to evaluate our individual and team performance during a game, we need five statisticians. One individual will keep the score book; another keeps the team performance chart. The other three statisticians keep the charts which make up the individual performance chart. These charts are a shot chart, a rebound-assist-draw, a charge chart, and a recovery-ball loss-defense error chart. Our managers will double as statisticians on game nights, and we will also have several individuals who are trained to be statisticians. Since we are now using video tape to record our games, we have the opportunity to get the entire game on tape. This gives us the opportunity to double check our statisticians. With the breakdown of our charts into manageable categories and the opportunity for a close check after most of our games, we now have an accurate method for measuring both individual and team performance.

THE INDIVIDUAL GAME PERFORMANCE CHART

The Individual Game Performance Chart is kept on all players who participate in the game. It records the individual player's performance in a number of categories and, from that performance, achieves a grade which indicates that player's performance score.

The chart (Diagram 8–1) is made up of the following categories: Field Goals Attempted, Field Goals Made; Free Throws Attempted, Free Throws Made; Offensive Rebounds, Defensive Rebounds; Assists; Draw a Charge; Recoveries; Ball Loss, which is divided into turn overs and violations; and Defense Errors. The Field Goals Attempted and Made are taken from the shot chart kept by one of our statisticians; the Free Throws Attempted and Made are taken from the score book; Offensive and Defensive Rebounds, Assists, and Draw a Charge are kept on one chart; Recoveries, Turnovers, Violations, and Defense Errors are kept on one chart.

Most of the categories are self-explanatory. The only two that require some elaboration are Recoveries and Defense Errors. A Recovery occurs any time one of our players gains possession of the basket-

INDIVIDUAL GAME PERFORMANCE

HARTLEY – VS – _____

AT _____ DATE _____

	1	2	3	4	OT	FINAL
HARTLEY						

PLAYER	FIELD GOALS		FREE THROWS		REBOUNDS		ASSISTS	DRAW A CHARGE	RECOV- ERY	BALL LOSS		DEF. ERROR	TOTAL POINTS	GAME PERF. SCORE
	ATT	MADE	ATT	MADE	OFF	DEF				TURN OVER	VIOLA- TION			
TOTALS														

Diagram 8-1

ball or does something to enable a teammate to gain possession, other than by a rebound. For example, if one of our player's tips a jump ball to a teammate, both players would get credit for a Recovery. If a player steals the basketball, intercepts a pass, or forces a turnover, then that player gets credit for a Recovery. A Defense Error is charged to one of our players when he violates one of our defensive principles, such as giving up the baseline, not blocking out, failing to deny the weakside flash, etc. The statistician who keeps the Recovery-Ball-Loss-Defense Error chart sits right behind the coaches so that they can tell him when to charge a defense error.

With these categories as a basis for individual player performance, the following grading system serves as an evaluation tool. Each category represents a plus or minus grade.

Made Field Goal	+2	Missed Field Goal	−1
Made Free Throw	+1	Missed Free Throw	−1
Rebound	+1	Ball Loss	−1
Assist	+1	Defense Error	−1
Recovery	+1		
Draw a Charge	+1		

Following a game, the statistics are taken from the various charts and checked against the video tape replay when it is available and then recorded in the Individual Game Performance Chart, and the player's grade is determined and recorded. The Individual Game Performance Chart in Diagram 8–2 depicts an actual game situation to illustrate the finished product. Taking player White as an example, we see that he made 10 field goals and one free throw, had four rebounds, five assists, and two recoveries for a plus total of 32. He also missed five field goal attempts, one free throw attempt, and committed two turnovers for a total of minus eight. Subtracting the minus eight from the plus 32 gives White the game performance score of +24.

Our coaches believe that this method of grading does a very good job of giving an overall picture of a player's performance during a game, because scoring alone is not the only means by which a high grade can be achieved. Using the same chart, we can look at player Boone as an example of this. The chart shows that he did not score during this game. He was 0 for 3 from the field, and attempted no free throws. However, he pulled down 11 rebounds, had six assists, and four recoveries. He thus had a total of minus three on the missed shots, but a total of plus 21 in the other categories, giving him a game per-

INDIVIDUAL GAME PERFORMANCE
HARTLEY – VS –
AT ST. JOHN ARENA DATE 3/22/

	1	2	3	4	OT	FINAL
HARTLEY	16	22	14	20		72
OPPONENTS	8	11	14	12		46

PLAYER	FIELD GOALS ATT	MADE	FREE THROWS ATT	MADE	REBOUNDS OFF	DEF	ASSISTS	DRAW A CHARGE	RECOV-ERY	BALL LOSS TURN-OVER	VIOLA-TION	DEF. ERROR	TOTAL POINTS	GAME PERF. SCORE
BOONE	3	0	0	0	4	7	6	0	4	0	0	0	0	+18
WHITE	15	10	2	1	1	3	5	0	2	2	0	0	21	+24
PROFERA	9	6	3	1	0	11	2	0	12	1	2	0	13	+30
GILLILAND	17	7	1	1	1	1	7	0	3	2	1	0	15	+14
JONES	16	8	1	0	1	1	5	0	3	2	1	0	16	+14
McNALLY, MARK	2	1	0	0	0	0	0	0	2	1	0	0	2	+2
WILE	1	1	2	1	0	0	0	0	2	0	0	0	3	+4
BENDER	2	0	3	2	0	1	0	0	1	0	0	0	2	+1
LONG	0	0	0	0	0	0	1	0	1	0	0	0	0	+2
McNALLY, MIKE	1	0	0	0	0	0	0	0	1	0	0	0	0	0
TOTALS	66	33	12	6	7	24	26	0	31	8	4	0	72	
	60%		50%											

Diagram 8-2

formance score of +18, despite the fact that he did not score a point. Scoring points, while obviously necessary for success, is not the sole criterion of the Game Performance Score.

This chart was developed to measure a player's total contribution during a game. I am sure all coaches could develop a chart which measures the areas that they want to know about and include other categories, but for the present we are satisfied with the Individual Game Performance Chart as we now use it.

We have used this basic grading format since 1965, and over that time we have developed a grading range which indicates a player's contribution. For a player who takes part in most of the game, at least three quarters, the following ratio between score and performance is:

0-5	poor performance
6-9	mediocre to average
10-15	solid performance
16-20	above average performance
21-29	excellent performance
30+	super performance

Looking back at the chart in Diagram 8–2, we see that our team received very solid performances from players Gilliland and Jones, and above average performance from Boone, and excellent performance from White, and a super performance from Profera. Profera was only the fourth leading scorer in the game, but his high shooting percentage along with his rebounding and recovery efforts indicate that he made a most significant contribution to the team in this particular game.

For substitutes, a different viewpoint must be used, since they will not usually have the same amount of playing time during the course of the game. If your sixth or seventh man does play quite a bit, then the above rating will hold, but if your substitutes are playing a quarter or less, then anytime they can be graded from a plus eight on up, they have done an exceptional job. If the substitute plays only briefly, then any kind of a plus score indicates some contribution to the total team effort.

The Individual Game Performance Chart has served as a very valuable tool for our coaching staff to achieve a better evaluation of individual performance after the game is over. Although nothing can be done about the preceding results, all coaches are aware that the major concern in our occupation is always getting ready for the next game. So this type of chart may give some information which will be useful in the weeks to come. As we know, most football coaches have very elaborate methods for grading their game films to determine individual performance. Basketball coaches can do the same thing so that they, too, can improve individual player performance. In fact, the basketball coach can grade his players much more easily than football coaches. He can devise statistical categories which can be recorded while the game is in progress and these categories can be interpreted immediately after the game. Thus, the basketball coach can grade his players even if films or video tape are unavailable. If these methods are available they can serve as a double check, but you will find that when statisticians are trained to keep a certain set of statistics, they will do a remarkably competent job. Grading individual performance is a good way for the coach to become aware of which players are performing capably, as well as showing which individuals need improvement. This factor can help the coach as a coach, and can also serve as a tool for motivation on the part of the individual players.

SEASON PERFORMANCE CHART

As the season progresses, we also keep a total game performance score on our players. This is done by filling out the Individual Game Performance Chart with the total account of the player's statistical achievements. Diagram 8–3 shows an example of this chart at the end of a season. The number of games played is placed to the left of the player's name, then his total statistics are filled in under each category, and the same grading method is used to calculate the season performance score. The players are ranked according to their performance score, since this is a more accurate appraisal of their overall contribution to the team than mere scoring statistics. As the above chart indicates, total contribution is a most important element in a team's success. For example, Profera was only the fourth leading scorer on this team, but his other statistical achievements made him the player with the highest performance score, a +536 for the season, which averages out to a game performance score of +20.6, indicating an above average performance throughout the season. Another example of total contribution is Boone, who was this team's sixth man for most of the season. His season performance score of +310, averages out to +12.4 per game, which is an indication that he made a remarkable contribution to

SEASON PERFORMANCE CHART

	1	2	3	4	OT	TOTAL	AVG
HARTLEY	397	477	445	486		1804	67.4
OPPONENTS	371	378	387	428		1564	60.2

PLAYER	FIELD GOALS		FREE THROWS		REBOUNDS		ASSISTS	DRAW A CHARGE	RECOV- ERY	BALL LOSS		DEF. ERROR	TOTAL PTS / SEASON PERF. AVG	SCORE
	ATT	MADE	ATT	MADE	OFF	DEF				TURN OVER	VIOLA- TION			
(26) PROFERA	210	117	77	48	82	156	62	4	131	31	22	6	282 / 10.8	+536
(25) WHITE	295	134	62	39	70	115	123	3	91	49	21	3	307 / 12.3	+464
(26) GILLILAND	404	197	98	73	14	30	117	6	120	65	38	3	467 / 17.9	+420
(24) McNALLY, MARK	237	105	34	23	54	101	78	4	80	28	15	7	233 / 8.9	+357
(25) BOONE	119	50	71	41	81	117	47	9	50	23	10	3	141 / 5.6	+310
(26) JONES	301	129	55	35	31	62	95	3	73	66	41	2	293 / 11.3	+257
(16) BENDER	18	8	7	5	7	10	9	1	4	1	0	1	21 / 1.3	+33
(21) WILE	8	4	12	6	2	5	7	1	13	5	5	0	14 / 0.7	+22
(15) McNALLY, MIKE	15	4	10	9	4	11	1	0	3	1	2	6	17 / 1.1	+21
(15) LONG	2	1	0	0	0	3	2	0	2	5	3	0	2 / 0.1	0
————	27	11	12	5	5	16	5	0	4	11	7	0	27 /	
TOTALS	1636	760	428	284	350	625	541	30	571	269	164	28		

Diagram 8-3

this team with his ability to come off the bench and play well.

These two charts, the Individual Game Performance Chart and the Season Performance Chart, are posted each Monday during the season so that each player can see his overall contribution to the team. It is considered more of an honor among our players to be the leader in performance score than to be just the leading scorer. This is an attitude which the coaches have consciously tried to develop, because we want players to realize that all phases of the game are important. They must work on all their skills to become as complete a basketball player as possible. We want players who will score when they have the opportunity, but will also hit the open man with the pass when he has a better opportunity. We want players who will work for the rebound, who will scramble for the loose basketball, who will stand their ground and take the charge. Players will do these things when they are convinced that these are the elements needed to build a successful basketball team. Keeping these charts is an indication to our players that the coaching staff is really interested in the various phases of the game and interested in keeping a tangible record of performance, a record that all can see, which measures the players' commitment to total performance,

If there is one characteristic which I would attach to the basketball teams which I have had the privilege to coach, it would be intensity of effort. I have sometimes been disappointed in our performance, but I have rarely been disappointed in the total effort put forth by the players. I would like to think that this characteristic is, in part, due to the emphasis our coaching staff places on total performance.

These charts not only provide a method of measuring performance, but they also serve as an incentive to our players. Even if the grading system is less than perfect, their incentive factor as a motivational tool makes the charts worthwhile.

THE TEAM OFFENSIVE PERFORMANCE CHART

We also keep a type of play by play chart for each game. This Team Offensive Performance Chart is depicted in Diagram 8–4. Comprised of one sheet for each quarter, each sheet has space for 25 possessions. We keep this chart for both our offense and defense but, since we are discussing offensive performance, the remarks will be limited to that phase of the chart.

For each possession, three columns of information are filled. The first column indicates the kind of offensive situation during that par-

| Quarter | 1 | 2 | 3 | 4 | | 242 |

Offense	Remarks	Result
SP FB P		
SP FB P		
SP FB P		
SP FB P		
SP FB P		
SP FB P		
SP FB P		
SP FB P		
SP FB P		
SP FB P		
SP FB P		
SP FB P		
SP FB P		
SP FB P		
SP FB P		
SP FB P		
SP FB P		
SP FB P		
SP FB P		
SP FB P		
SP FB P		
SP FB P		
SP FB P		
SP FB P		

| Possessions | Points | PPP |

Diagram 8–4

ticular possession. The SP stands for set pattern and the number next to it tells us which pattern was being executed. The offensive numbering code is as follows:

1   Regular Man to Man
2   Reverse Man to Man
3   Invert Man to Man
4   Mirror Offense Variation

5   Guard Around
6   Guard In
7   Wing Over
8   Regular Zone Offense
9   Overload Zone Offense
#10   Control Offense
#11   Freeze Offense
#12   Stall Offense
#13   Zone Out of Bounds Play
#14   Man Out of Bounds Play

The FB is for Fast Break, the P represents our Offense against a press. The second column for Remarks is where the statistician charts the game. In this column, everything which happens during a possession is charted. This will include the number of the player who shoots the ball and the type of shot which is taken. For example, #20 LU (lay up); RCJ (right corner jump shot); LWJ (left wing jump shot); FLJ (foul line jump shot); TP (tip in); REB (rebound), etc. As previously stated, everything which occurs during a possession is charted, so for example, #20 FLJ, 50 TP would indicate that #20 shot a jump shot from the foul line, missed the shot, but it was tipped in by #50. The remarks column also tells us what happened if we do not get a shot off. For example, #22 BP (bad pass); Trav. (travel); 3 sec. (Three seconds); CH (charging foul), etc. If a player is fouled, this is noted and recorded as in the scorebook, #52 fouled by #33. The three point play would be indicated by #42 LU fouled by #21. The last column on the chart simply indicates the result of each possession by indicating the number of points scored, 0, 1, 2, 3, etc.

The statistician who keeps this chart must be well trained and must sit behind the coaches, so that one of the assistants can tell him which patterns are being used. We also want the statistician to record the time on each possession when it is feasible to do so, e.g., after a basket is scored, when a foul shot is being attempted, etc. At the end of the quarter, the statistician fills in the categories at the bottom of the chart. These categories are Possessions, Points Scored, and Percentage. The percentage is the category which gives us a grade for the offensive performance during that quarter, and it is calculated by dividing the points scored by the number of possessions. For example, a quarter in which a team had 18 possessions and scored 16 points would result in a percentage grade of 94%.

Quarter ① 2 3 4

Offense	Remarks		Result
/ ⓈⓅ FB P	42 FLJ	7:50	2
/ ⓈⓅ FB P	52 RCJ 40 REB		0
/ ⓈⓅ FB P	22 RWJ	7:00	2
/ ⓈⓅ FB P	22 BP		0
/ ⓈⓅ FB P	32 TRAV	6:05	0
/ ⓈⓅ FB P	22 LWJ	5:38	2
/4 ⓈⓅ FB P	42 LU	5:04	2
/ ⓈⓅ FB P	32 RWJ	4:36	2
/ ⓈⓅ FB P	32 FUM		0
/ ⓈⓅ FB P	FOUL 23-32 ⊗ O	3:36	1
/ ⓈⓅ FB P	32 OFF. FOUL	2:56	0
/ ⓈⓅ FB P	22 LWJ		0
/ ⓈⓅ FB P	FOUL 53-52 ⊗ O	1:59	1
SP ⒻⒷ P	22 LU		0
/ ⓈⓅ FB P	32 LWJ	:57	2
SP ⒻⒷ P	42 LU	:45	2
SP ⒻⒷ P	22 LU	:30	2
SP ⒻⒷ P	40 LWJ	:01	2
SP FB P			
SP FB P			
SP FB P			
SP FB P			
SP FB P			
SP FB P			

Possessions	Points	PPP
18	20	1.10

Diagram 8–5

Diagram 8–5 is an example of one actual quarter of play as kept on the Team Offensive Performance Chart. The #1 next to SP indicates that the Regular Man to Man Offense was being used. In this particular quarter the pattern was executed 13 times and resulted in 12 points. The chart also shows that we had four fast break opportunities from which we scored six points. On our seventh possession, the chart indicates that we scored on a baseline out of bounds play against a man to man defense.

TEAM OFFENSIVE PERFORMANCE GRADE	1	2	3	4	OT	TOTALS
POSSESSIONS	20	20	19	21		80
POINTS	19	20	24	22		85
POINTS PER POSSESSION	.91	1.00	1.20	1.05		1.06

Diagram 8–6

In addition to the scoring information, the chart also shows that we took 13 shots and made nine, were two of four from the free throw line, had one offensive rebound, and turned the basketball over four times. Finally, at the bottom of the chart is the offensive grade for that quarter, which in this case was a very outstanding effort of 110%.

At the end of the game, the statistician totals each quarter of the Team Offensive Performance Chart and records the grade on a grade sheet, an example of which is shown in Diagram 8–6.

USE OF THE TEAM OFFENSIVE PERFORMANCE CHART

After the statisticians have turned in all their charts, the coaches then double check them by means of the video tape replay, when it is available, and then fill in a set of charts which become part of a permanent file.

The Team Offensive Performance Chart is broken down into the various offensive categories so that the coaches can ascertain a more in-depth picture of just how our points are being scored, which patterns are achieving results, whether the fast break is being productive, and what kinds of turnovers are being committed, and by whom. Diagram 8–7 shows an example of how we break down the Team Offensive Performance Chart.

This type of chart gives the coach a clearer picture of just how his offense performed during the course of a game. The example shows a wide open basketball game, in which three different set patterns were run a total of 32 times and produced 28 points.

This is further broken down so that it can be noted that the Regular Zone Offense was used 16 times in the first half and resulted in 18 points, while in the second half of the game the opponents went to a man to man defense in the front court, and we responded by using the

QT	PATTERN POSS-PTS-PPP	FAST BREAK POSS-PTS-PPP	PRESS OFF. POSS-PTS-PPP	OUT OF BDS. POSS PTS PPP	BAD PASS	FUM.	STEAL	3 SEC	TRAV	OFF FOUL	OTHER VIOL
1	REG. ZONE 9-14 1.56	11-9 .82	2-2 1.00		2			1	2		
2	REG. ZONE 7-4 .57	8-10 1.25	9-6 .67		3				2		
3	GD. AROUND 6-2 .33	10-12 1.20	5-6 1.20		2	2			2		
4	REG. MAN 10-8 .80	7-5 .71	3-2 .67	2-2 1.00	1						
T O T A L S	REG. ZONE 16-18 1.12 GD. AROUND 6-2 .33 REG. MAN 10-8 .80 _____ 32-28 .88	36-36 1.00	19-16 .84	2-2 1.00	8	2	1	2	6		

Diagram 8–7

Guard Around Pattern in the third quarter, and the Regular Man to Man Offense in the last quarter. In this game, our team had 36 fast break situations which resulted in 36 points, and there were 19 possessions against a pressing defense in which 16 points were scored. Next to each pattern breakdown goes a percentage grade to indicate the effectiveness of the offense.

At the bottom of the chart the various categories are totaled and a percentage grade is recorded which will coincide with the grade on the Team Offensive Performance Chart. In this case, the grade of 94% is a very good offensive performance grade. This breakdown chart also shows that our team committed 19 turnovers, the most common being the bad pass and the traveling violation. Since this was a very fast paced game, a high number of turnovers must be expected, especially when there is a great deal of fast breaking. Since we scored one point for every fast break and our defense played quite well, the turnovers were not a significant factor in our 84-63 victory. Most of our games are not quite as wide open, but this game serves as a good example for the break down chart since a variety of offensive attacks were used because of the various types of defenses employed by our opponents.

EVALUATING TEAM PERFORMANCE

At the conclusion of the game a team performance grade is arrived at by dividing the total number of points scored by the total number of possessions. This figure then represents the Team Offensive Performance Grade. From our experience with this type of grading system over the past several seasons we have compiled the following grading range:

Below 69%	Poor Performance
70%-80%	Average Performance
81%-90%	Above Average Performance
91%-99%	Excellent Performance
100%	Super Performance

The grading standards can be easily raised or lowered depending on the level of competition. In our situation, we have found that our basketball team must consistently grade in the 75-90% range if we are to win basketball games. Our five most successful basketball teams had yearly offensive performance grades of 89%, 86%, 88%, 89%, and 87%.

POST SEASON CHARTS

At the end of the season, the Team Offensive Performance Chart is reviewed and a master chart is compiled. In this master chart we list all the offensive situations encountered during the season, break down all the patterns into possessions and points scored, and then grade each category as a guide to indicate its effectiveness during the season. Diagram 8–8 is an example of this master chart from 18 games.

This chart shows that this particular team was exceptional with the fast break and was extremely effective against zone defenses. The chart also indicates that the Regular Man to Man Offense and the Guard Around were effective enough so that the other variations were not used very much. This team also did an excellent job with the delay game, which is an indication that they not only got open shots, but that they were able to hit the free throws during the delay situation.

This chart by no means tells the entire story of a season as far as the effectiveness of a pattern is concerned, but it does serve as a guideline. In the chart, for example, both the Reverse and Invert Man to Man Offenses show only an average grade when compared with the other man to man patterns, but I can recall that during that season the Reverse and Invert Offenses produced several key baskets in two very important victories. So the master chart gives us a general overview of our offensive performance, but we realize that the various patterns which we have in our offensive system each has a definite purpose, depending on the defense of the opponents, and so each pattern will have to fulfill its particular purpose during the course of a season if we are to

OFFENSE	POSS	PTS	P.P.P.
REGULAR MAN TO MAN	351	310	.88
REVERSE MAN TO MAN	63	38	.72
INVERT MAN TO MAN	76	57	.75
GUARD AROUND	180	167	.93
REGULAR ZONE	225	215	.96
OVERLOAD ZONE	164	150	.91
FAST BREAK	247	268	1.08
CONTROL - STALL - FREEZE	32	31	.97
PRESS OFFENSE	65	56	.86
SIDELINE OUT OF BOUNDS	18	12	.80
BASELINE OUT OF BOUNDS	40	35	.87
EMERGENCY SCORE	0	0	0
	1451	1339	.92

TURNOVERS					
BAD PASS	FUMBLE	STEAL	VIOLATION	OFF. FOUL	TO/PCT
130	34	20	115	19	318/22%

Diagram 8–8

be successful in establishing the concept of court control.

At the bottom of the master chart is the listing of the kinds of turnovers we had while running our offensive system (refer to Diagram 8–8). This set of statistics is tied in with the offensive patterns as a way of checking on how the turnovers affected the offensive performance of our basketball team. During this 18 game schedule the turnovers amounted to 318, with bad passes and violations leading the way. As indicated by the chart, this team did a great deal of fast breaking and turnovers must be expected to occur. Looking at the turnover situation in more detail, we see that these 318 turnovers occurred out of 1451 offensive possessions, or in other words we turned the basketball over 22% of the time. Looking at this statistic from a positive viewpoint, this means that we were able to execute our patterns almost eight out of ten times without a turnover. Our experience has shown that if we can keep the turnover percentage at less than 25% of our offensive possessions, then we are playing good offensive basketball. Again, I want to point out that this is a relative percentage based on our style of play and so could be raised or lowered depending on different levels or styles of play.

THE VALUE OF STATISTICS

Our coaching staff believes that the variety of charts we use serves a worthwhile purpose. Not only do they indicate adequacies and deficiencies to the coaches but they also create interest among the players. Basketball players, just like students in the classroom, want to know how they are measuring up, and our approach is to show them just exactly how they are measuring up in their individual and team performance. In this way, we have a tool, not only for grading, but also for motivation.

These statistics can be used to indicate just how much one is contributing to the team. For example, the player who may only be scoring four points a game, but is grabbing 15 rebounds or getting eight assists will see from his individual grade that he is contributing.

Statistics can be used to indicate anything a coach wants them to indicate. We see them as a method of producing a capsule view of individual and team performance and as a method for motivation and encouragement. Creating the atmosphere in which the player knows that he will be credited for his all around good play, or encouraged to improve his shortcomings makes the player aware that the coaching staff is interested in him as an individual. This kind of awareness encourages a better effort from week to week, and as the better effort brings improved performance, the better your chances of establishing full court control become.

INDEX